Children's Favorites

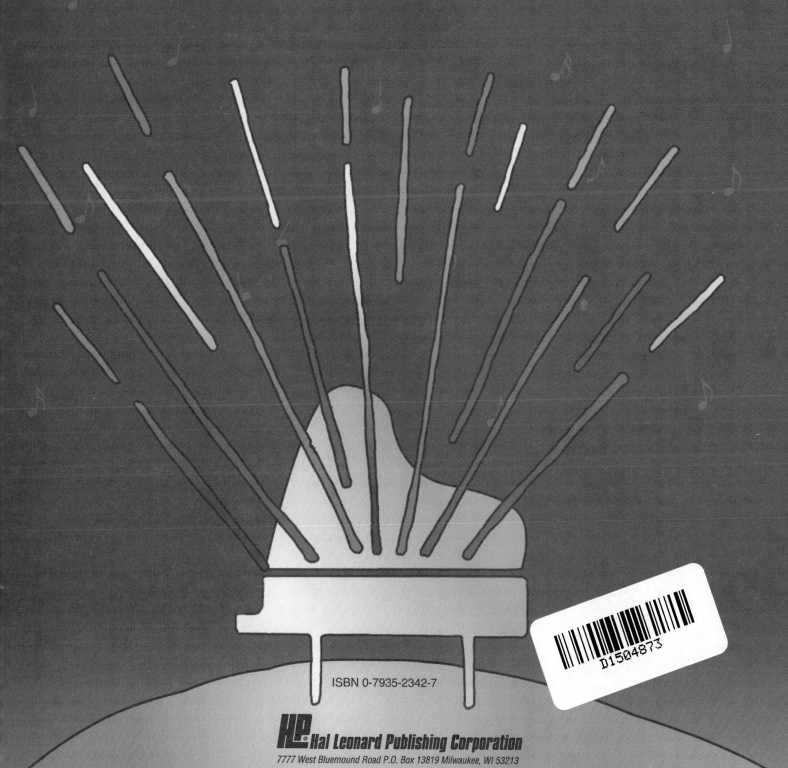

ISBN 0-7935-2342-7

HP Hal Leonard Publishing Corporation
7777 West Bluemound Road P.O. Box 13819 Milwaukee, WI 53213

D1504873

Children's Favorites

A-TISKET A-TASKET

Moderately

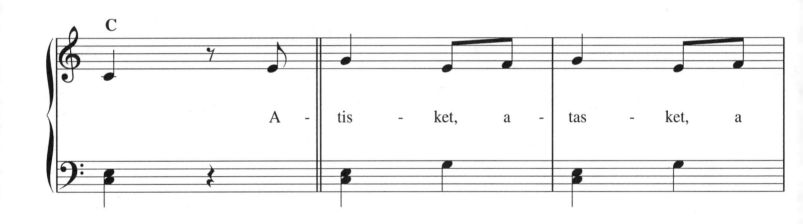

A - tis - ket, a - tas - ket, a

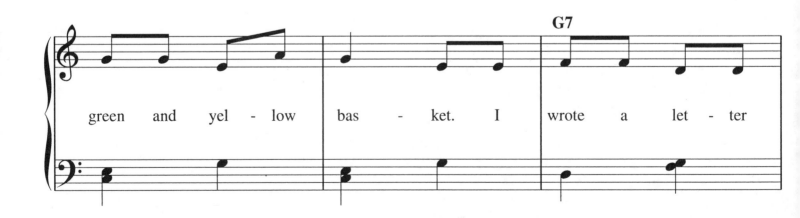

green and yel - low bas - ket. I wrote a let - ter

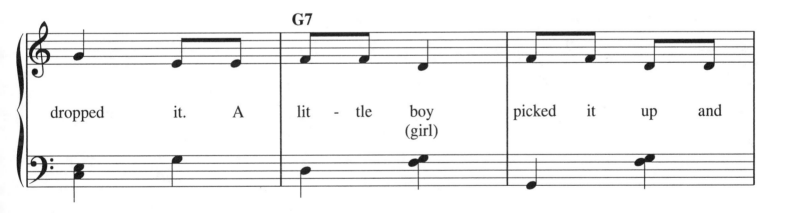

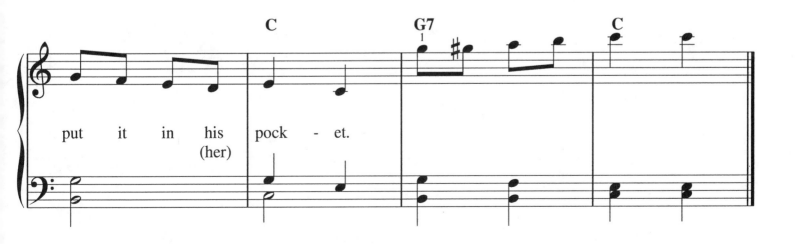

ABC-DEF-GHI

March Tempo

Words by JOE RAPOSO and JON STONE
Music by JOE RAPOSO

AB - C - DEF - GHI - J - KL - M - NOP - QR - STUV - WX - YZ___

___ is the most re-mark-a-ble word I've ev-er seen.

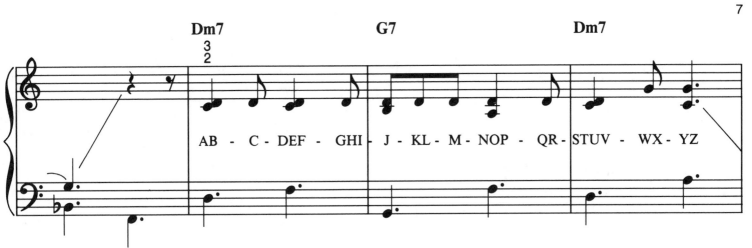

AB - C - DEF - GHI - J - KL - M - NOP - QR - STUV - WX - YZ

I wish I knew ex - act - ly what I mean.

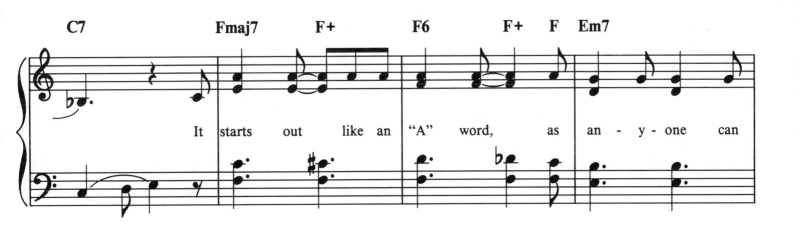

It starts out like an "A" word, as an - y - one can

see, _____ but some - where there in the mid - dle, it gets

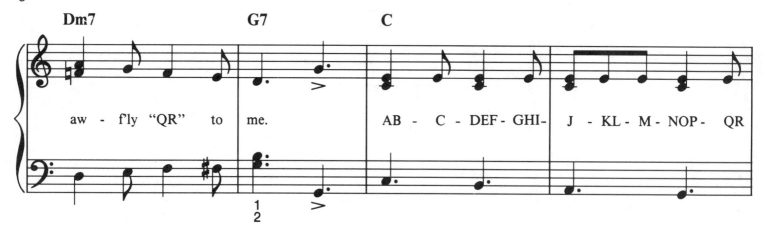

aw - f'ly "QR" to me. AB - C - DEF - GHI- J - KL - M - NOP - QR

STUV - WX- YZ! If I ev - er find out just what this word can

mean I'll be the smart - est bird the world has ev - er

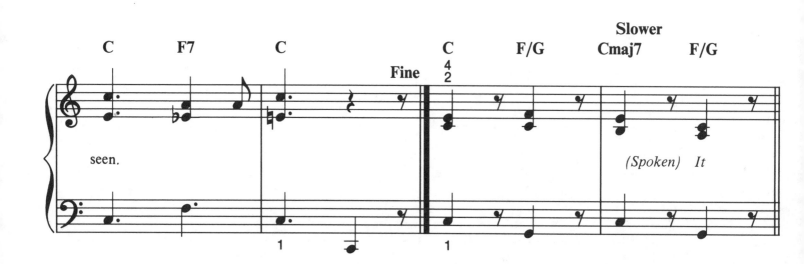

seen. (Spoken) It

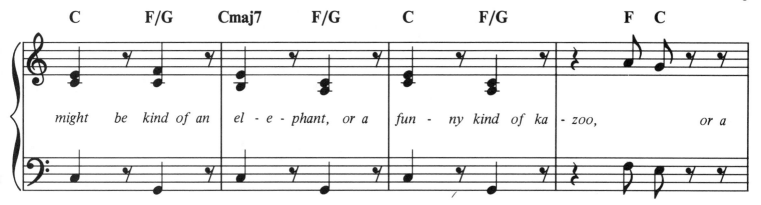

might be kind of an el - e - phant, or a fun - ny kind of ka - zoo, or a

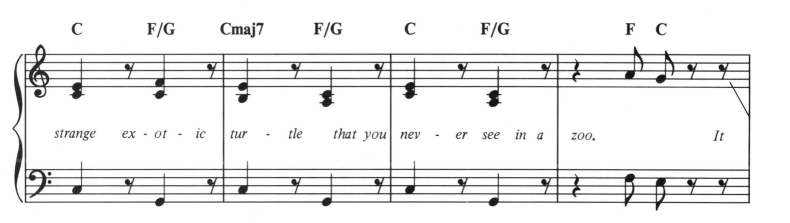

strange ex - ot - ic tur - tle that you nev - er see in a zoo. It

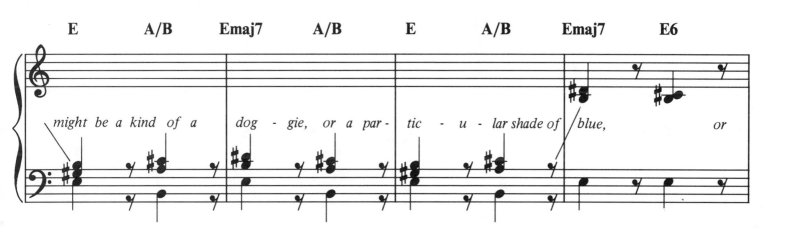

might be a kind of a dog - gie, or a par - tic - u - lar shade of blue, or

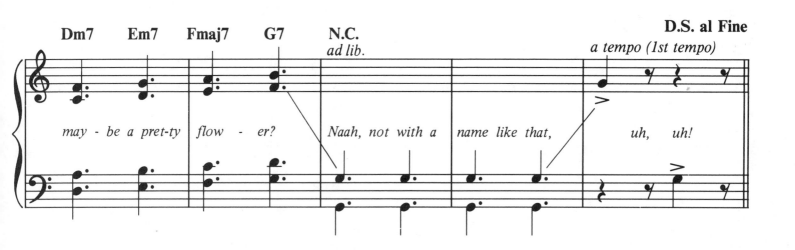

D.S. al Fine

a tempo (1st tempo)

ad lib.

may - be a pret - ty flow - er? Naah, not with a name like that, uh, uh!

ANIMAL FAIR

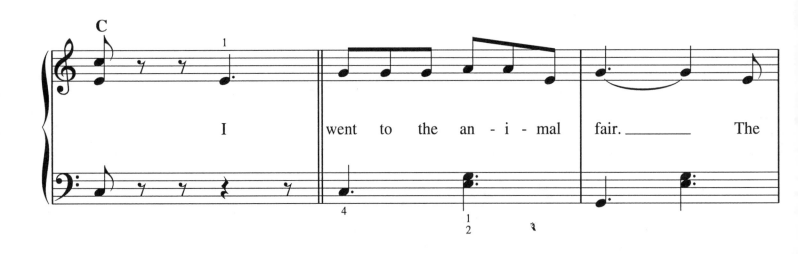

I went to the an-i-mal fair._____ The

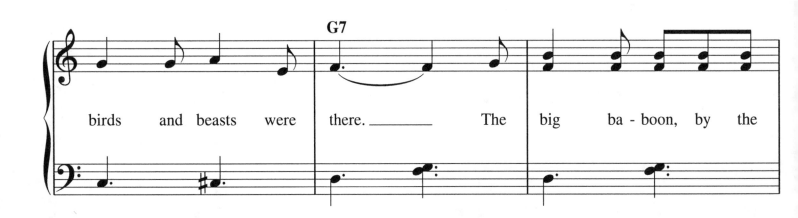

birds and beasts were there._____ The big ba-boon, by the

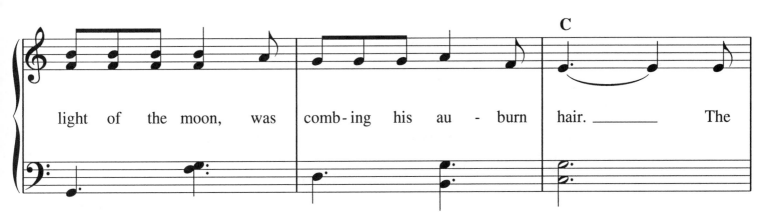

light of the moon, was comb-ing his au - burn hair. _____ The

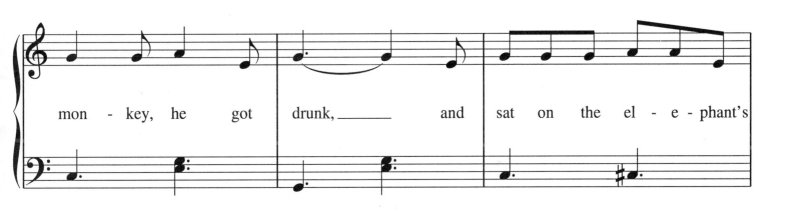

mon - key, he got drunk, _____ and sat on the el - e - phant's

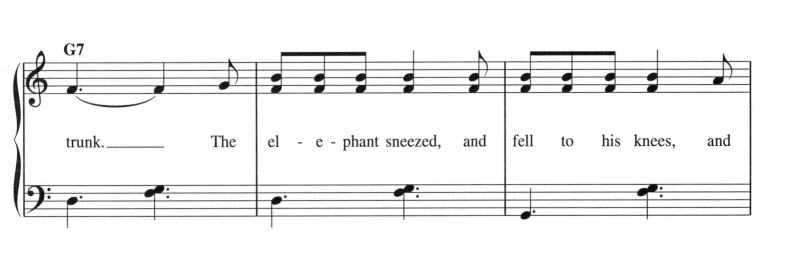

trunk. _____ The el - e - phant sneezed, and fell to his knees, and

what be - came of the monk, the monk, the monk, the monk?

BINGO

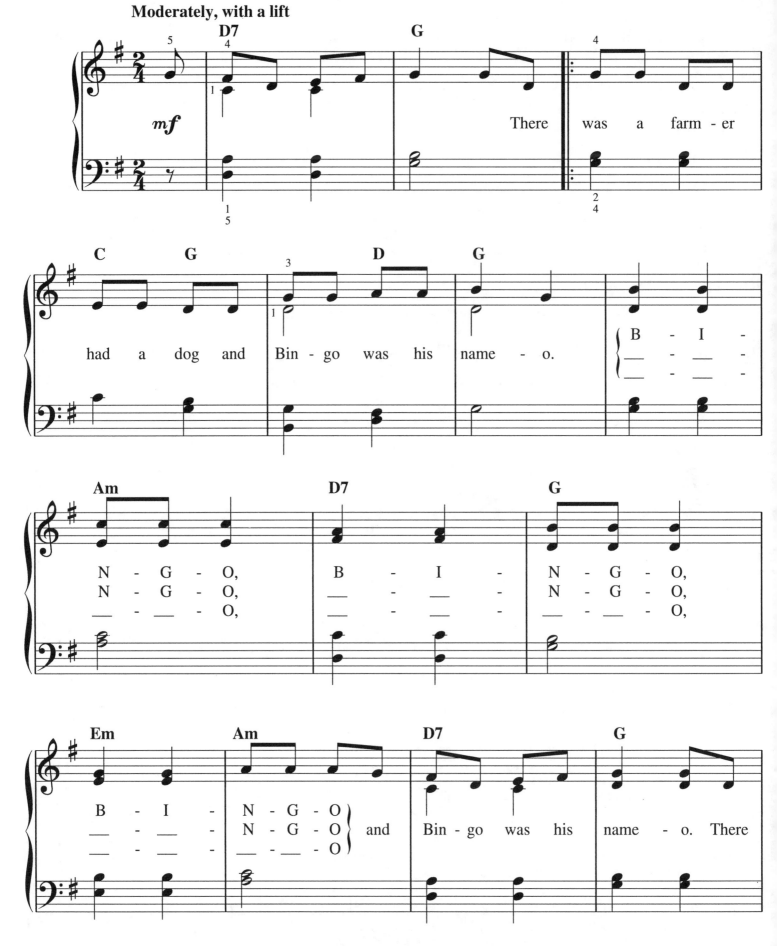

THE BEAR WENT OVER THE MOUNTAIN

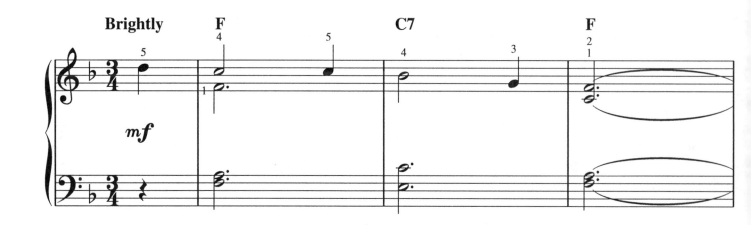

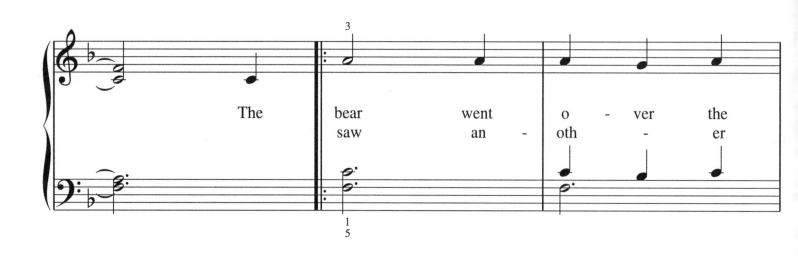

The
bear went o - ver the
saw an - oth - er

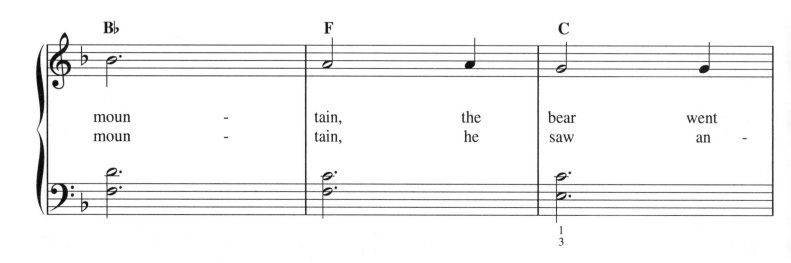

moun - tain, the bear went
moun - tain, he saw an -

BEIN' GREEN

Words and Music by
JOE RAPOSO

Cmaj7   **B7#5**

eas - y   be - in' green,   it seems you blend in with so man - y oth - er

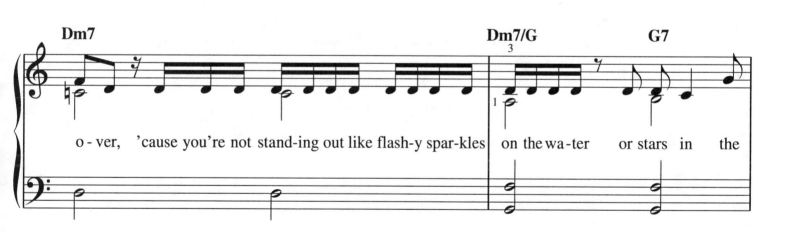

Gm6/B♭   **A7sus**   **A7**

or - di - nar - y things,   and peo - ple tend to pass you

Dm7   **Dm7/G**   **G7**

o - ver,   'cause you're not stand-ing out like flash-y spar-kles on the wa-ter   or stars in   the

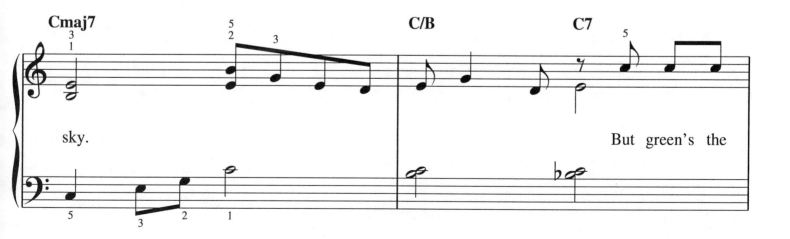

Cmaj7   **C/B**   **C7**

sky.   But green's the

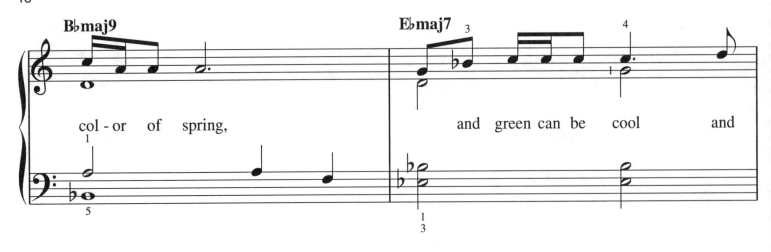

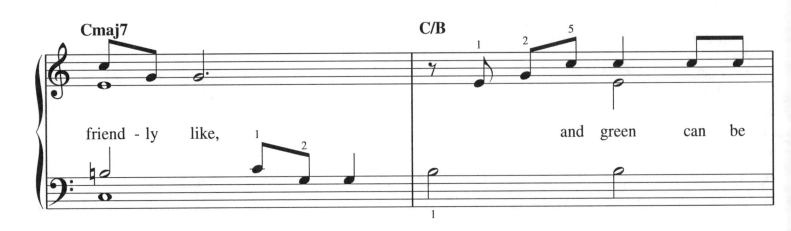

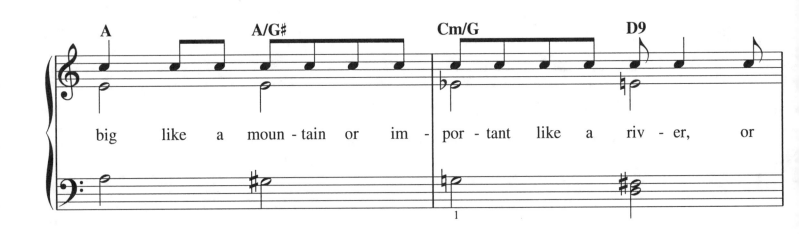

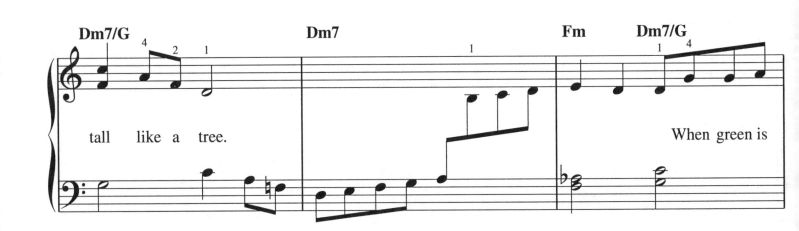

"C" IS FOR COOKIE

Words and Music by
JOE RAPOSO

With a jiggle and a bounce

C is for Cook-ie, that's good e-nough for me!
(Spoken) A round cook-ie with one bite out of it looks like a C.

C is for Cook-ie, that's good e-nough for me!
A round doughnut with one bite out of it also looks like a C.

To Coda ⊕

C   is   for Cook - ie,   that's | good e - nough for   me!   Oh,
But   it   is   not   as   good as | a   cookie. Oh,   and   the

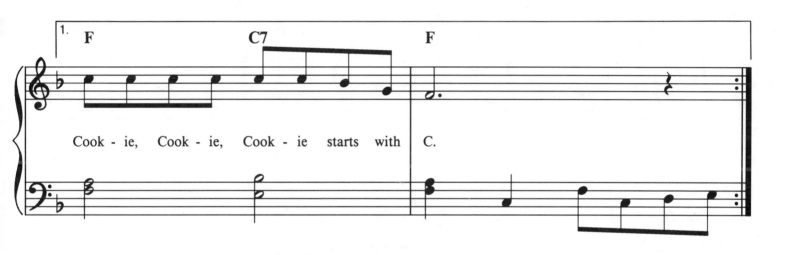

Cook - ie,   Cook - ie,   Cook - ie   starts with | C.

D.S. al Coda
(first lyric)

moon sometimes looks like   a   C,   but   you | can't eat that!   (Sung) So

CODA ⊕

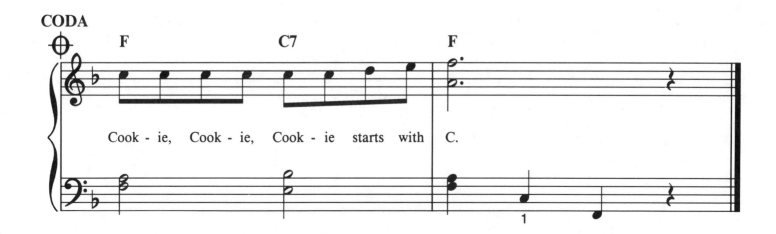

Cook - ie,   Cook - ie,   Cook - ie   starts with | C.

DO-RE-MI
(From "THE SOUND OF MUSIC")

Lyrics by OSCAR HAMMERSTEIN II
Music by RICHARD RODGERS

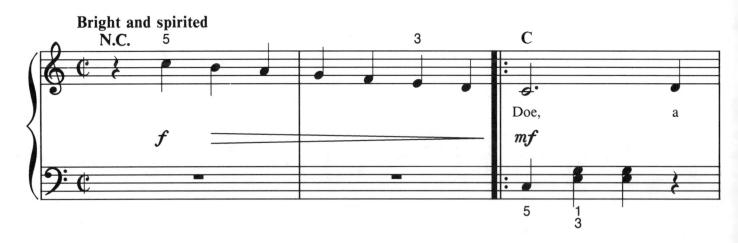

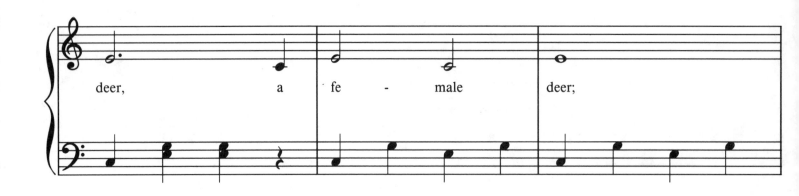

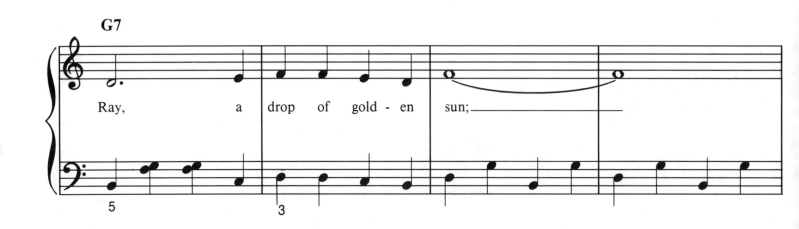

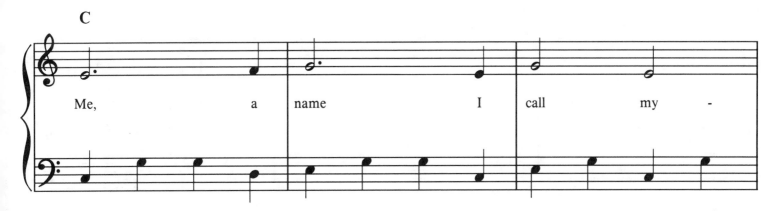

Me, a name I call my -

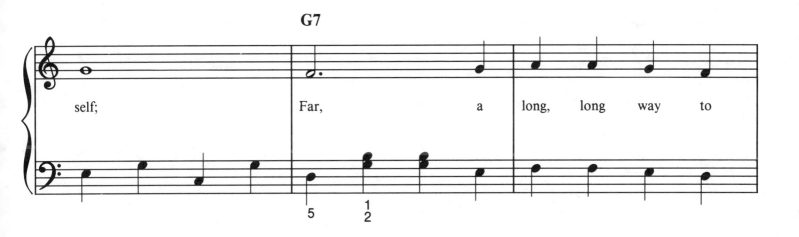

self; Far, a long, long way to

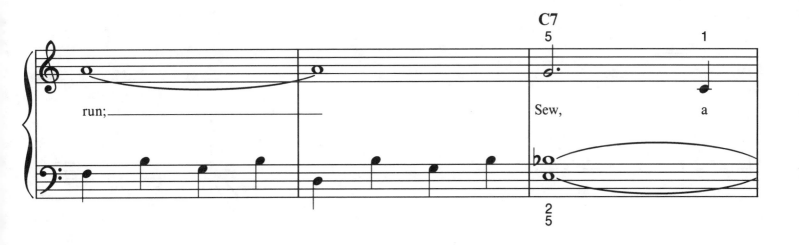

run; Sew, a

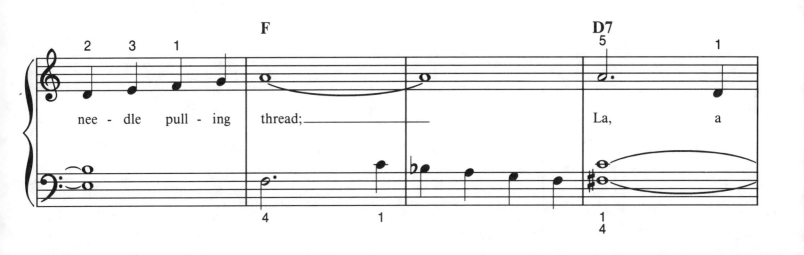

nee - dle pull - ing thread; La, a

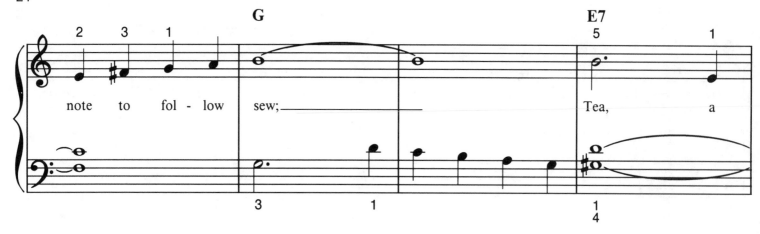

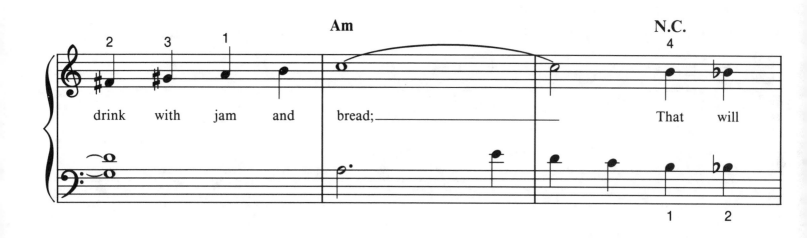

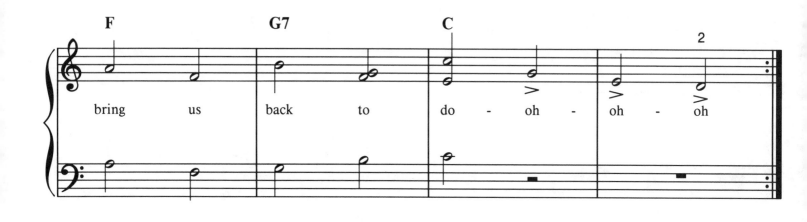

DOWN BY THE STATION

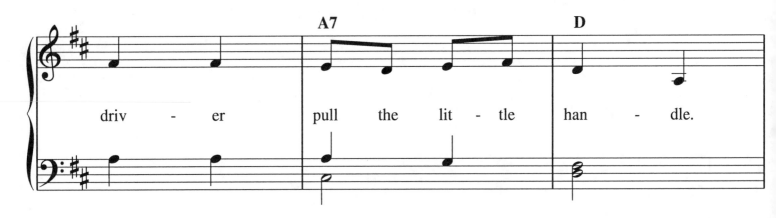

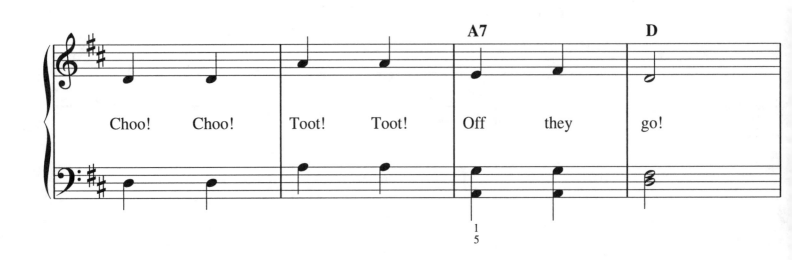

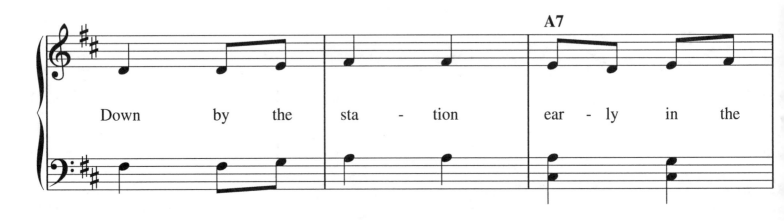

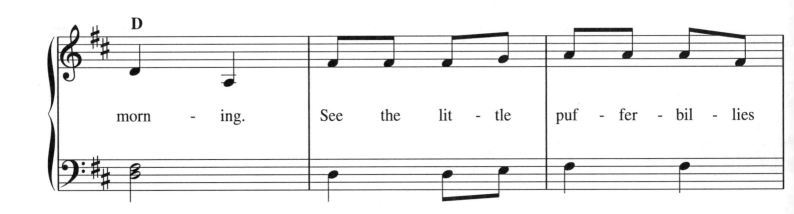

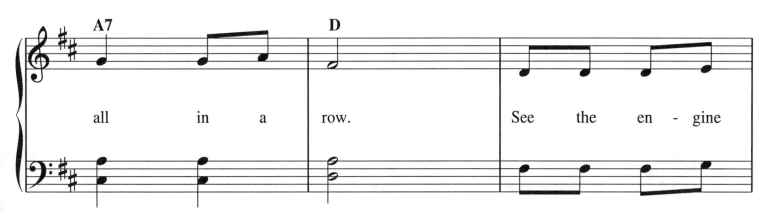

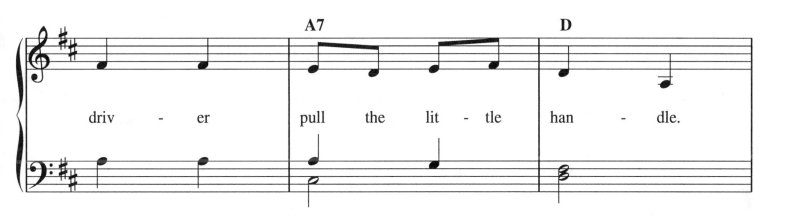

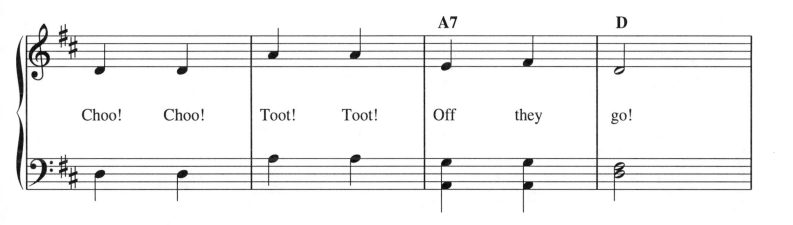

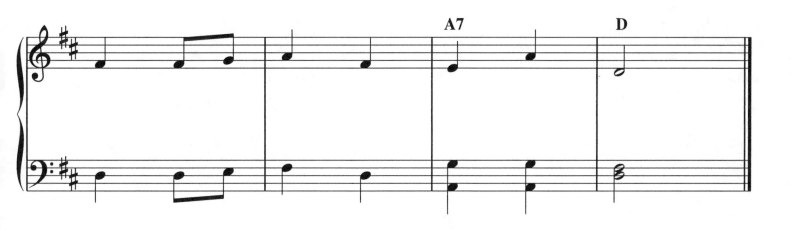

EENCY WEENCY SPIDER

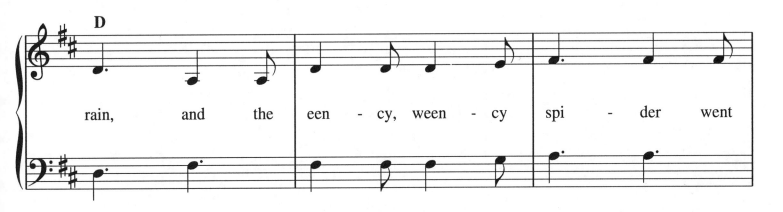

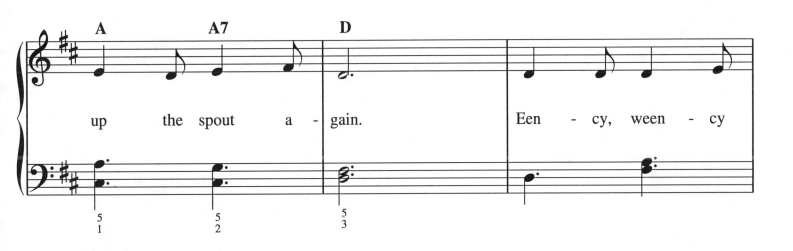

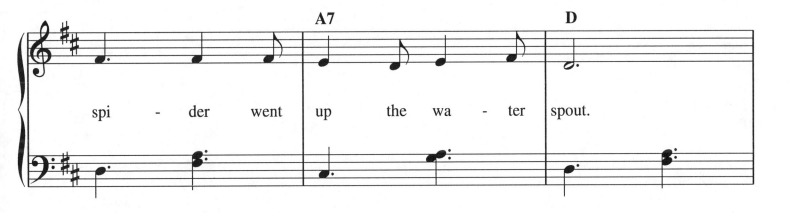

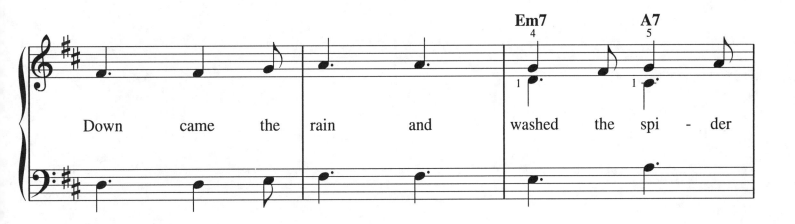

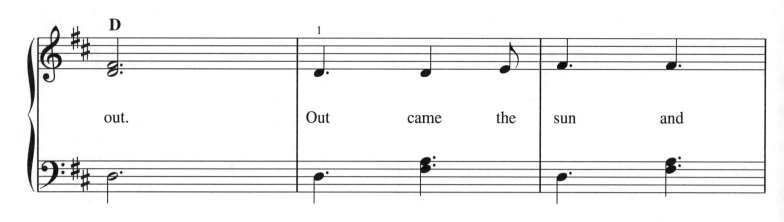

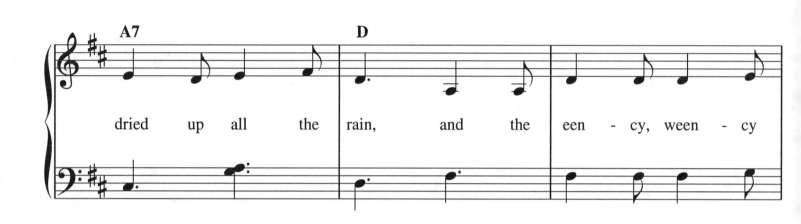

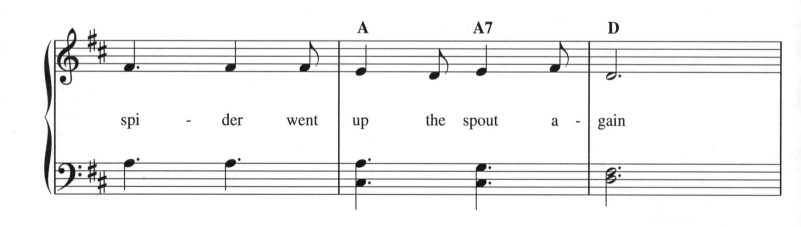

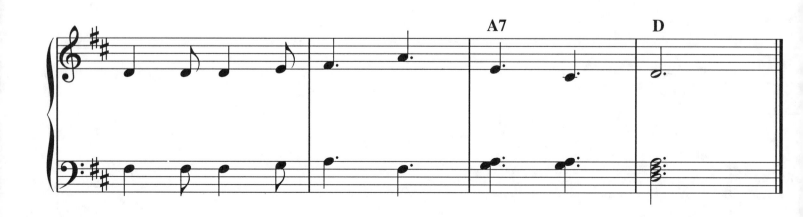

FROGGIE WENT A-COURTIN'

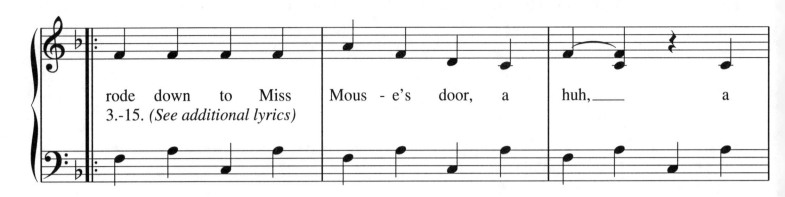

rode down to Miss | Mous - e's door, a | huh, _____ a

3.-15. *(See additional lyrics)*

huh. _____ Well, he | rode down to Miss | Mous - e's door, where

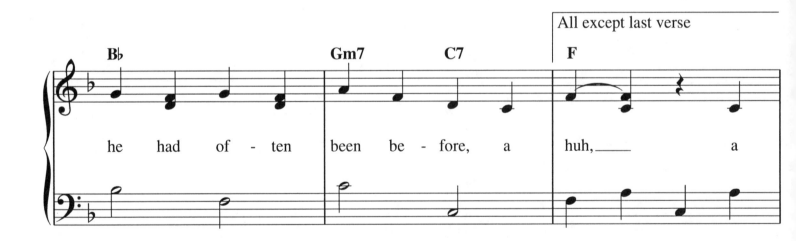

B♭ | | **Gm7** **C7** | All except last verse **F**

he had of - ten | been be - fore, a | huh, _____ a

| Last verse **F**

huh. He | huh, _____ a | huh.

Additional Lyrics

3. He took Miss Mousie on his knee, a-huh, a-huh,
   He took Miss Mousie on his knee,
   Said, "Miss Mousie will you marry me?" A-huh, a-huh.

4. "I'll have to ask my Uncle Rat, etc.
   See what he will say to that.", etc.

5. "Without my Uncle Rat's consent,
   I would not marry the President."

6. Well, Uncle Rat laughed and shook his fat sides,
   To think his niece would be a bride.

7. Well, Uncle Rat rode off to town
   To buy his niece a wedding gown.

8. "Where will the wedding supper be?"
   "Way down yonder in a hollow tree."

9. "What will the wedding supper be?"
   "A fried mosquito and a roasted flea."

10. First to come in were two little ants,
    Fixing around to have a dance.

11. Next to come in was a bumble bee,
    Bouncing a fiddle on his knee.

12. Next to come in was a fat sassy lad,
    Thinks himself as big as his dad.

13. Thinks himself a man indeed,
    Because he chews the tobacco weed.

14. And next to come in was a big tomcat,
    He swallowed the frog and the mouse and the rat.

15. Next to come in was a big old snake,
    He chased the party into the lake.

THE FARMER IN THE DELL

farm - er takes a wife. Heigh - ho, the

der - ry o! The farm - er takes a wife.

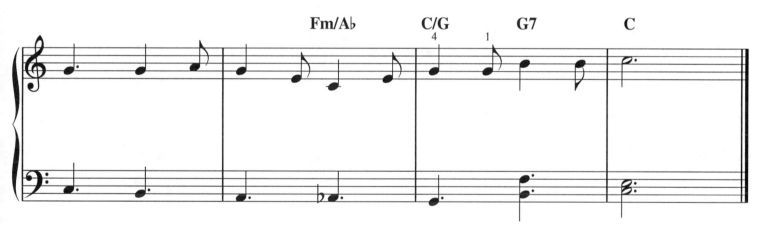

Additional Lyrics

3. The wife takes the child,
   The wife takes the child,
   Heigh-ho, the derry o!
   The wife takes the child.

4. The child takes the nurse,
   The child takes the nurse,
   Heigh-ho, the derry o!
   The child takes the nurse.

5. The nurse takes the dog,
   The nurse takes the dog,
   Heigh-ho, the derry o!
   The nurse takes the dog.

6. The dog takes the cat,
   The dog takes the cat,
   Heigh-ho, the derry o!
   The dog takes the cat.

7. The cat takes the rat,
   The cat takes the rat,
   Heigh-ho, the derry o!
   The cat takes the rat.

8. The rat takes the cheese,
   The rat takes the cheese,
   Heigh-ho, the derry o!
   The rat takes the cheese.

9. The cheese stands alone,
   The cheese stands alone,
   Heigh-ho, the derry o!
   The cheese stands alone.

FRÈRE JACQUES

Happily

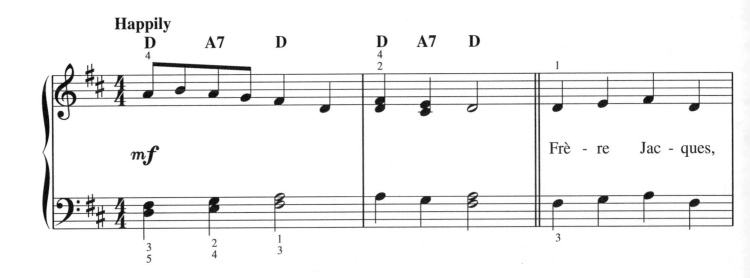

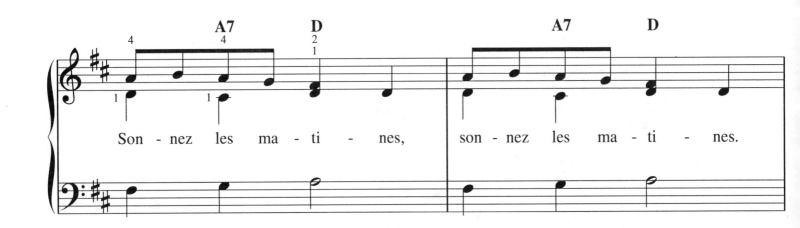

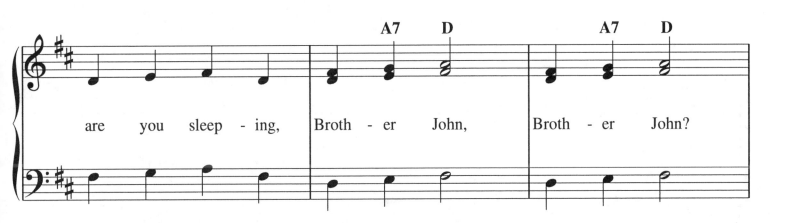

GETTING TO KNOW YOU

(From "THE KING AND I")

Lyrics by OSCAR HAMMERSTEIN II
Music by RICHARD RODGERS

get - ting to hope you like me.

Get - ting to know you,

put - ting it my way, but nice - ly,

you are pre - cise - ly my cup of

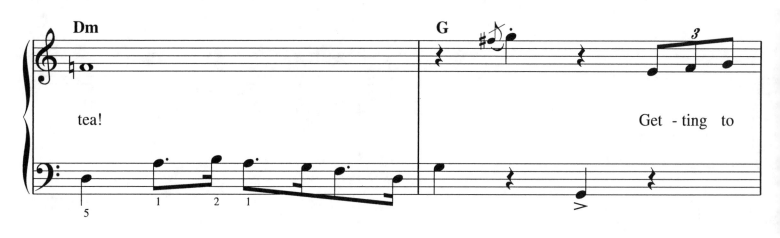

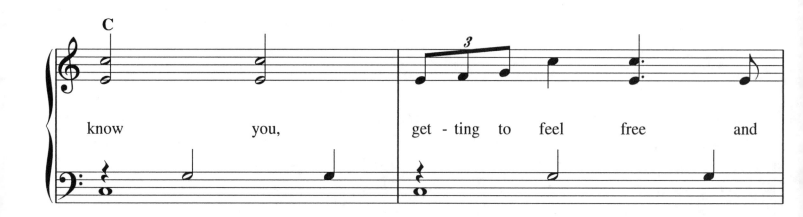

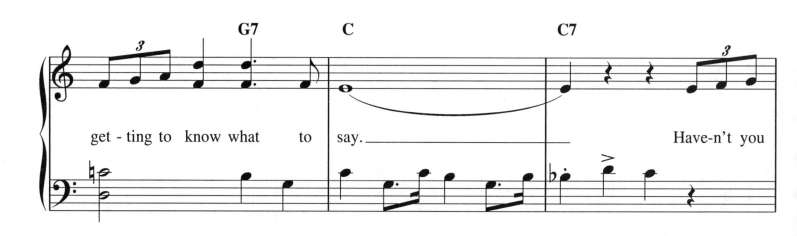

GO IN AND OUT THE WINDOW

Brightly

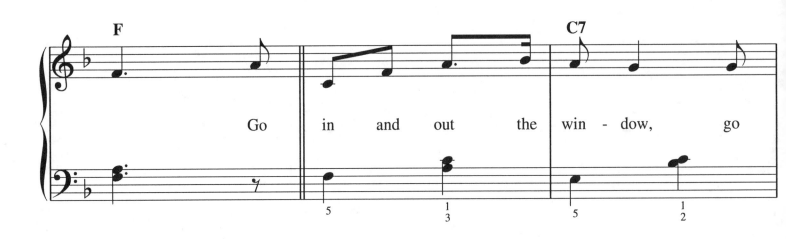

Go in and out the win - dow, go

in and out the win - dow, go in and out the

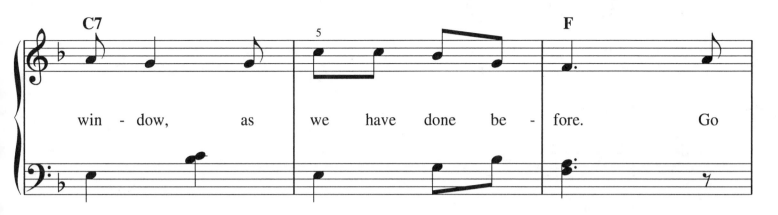

win - dow, as we have done be - fore. Go

forth and choose your part - ner, go forth and choose your

part - ner, go forth and choose your part - ner, as

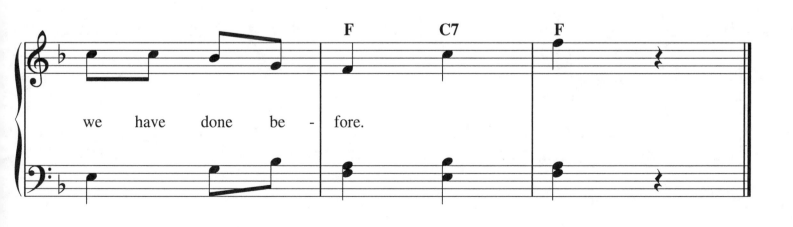

we have done be - fore.

HICKORY DICKORY DOCK

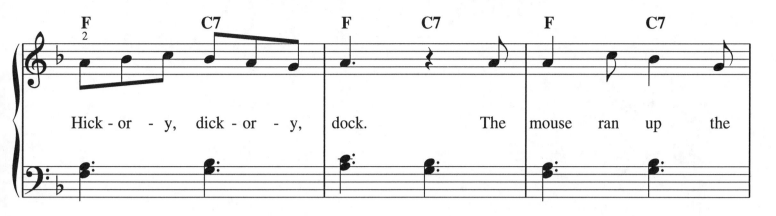

Hick - or - y, dick - or - y, dock. The mouse ran up the

clock. The clock struck one, the mouse ran down,

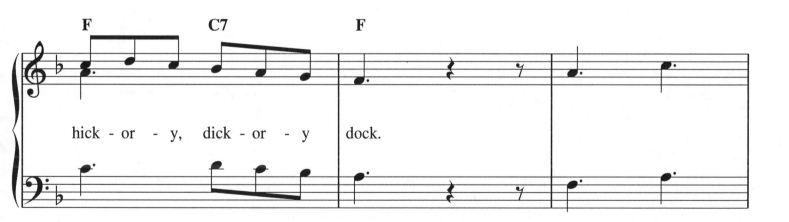

hick - or - y, dick - or - y dock.

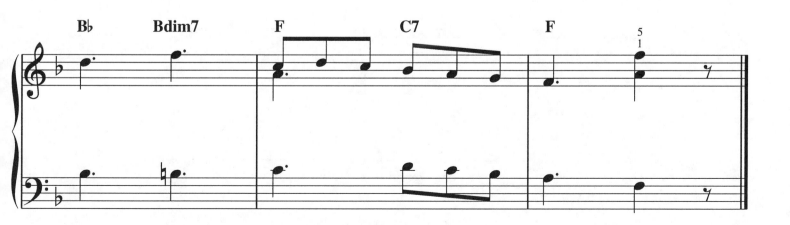

HUMPTY DUMPTY

Hump - ty Dump - ty sat on a

wall. Hump - ty Dump - ty had a great

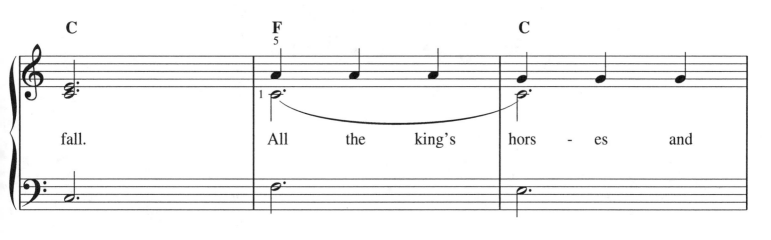

fall.　　　　　All　　the　　king's　　hors - es　　and

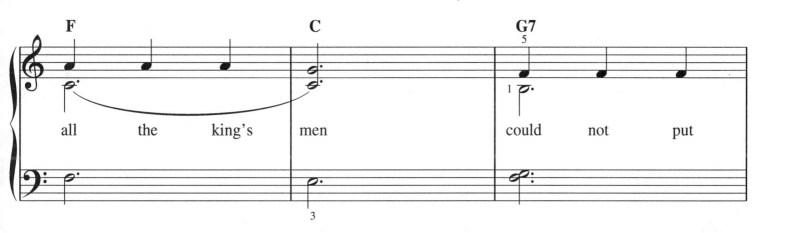

all　　the　　king's　　men　　　　could　　not　　put

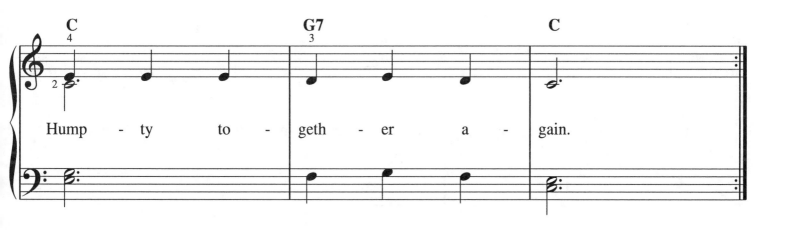

Hump - ty　　to - geth - er　　a - gain.

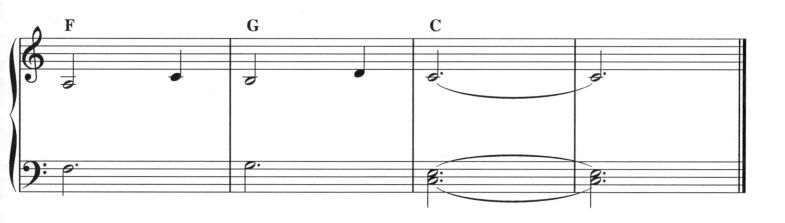

I'VE BEEN WORKING ON THE RAILROAD

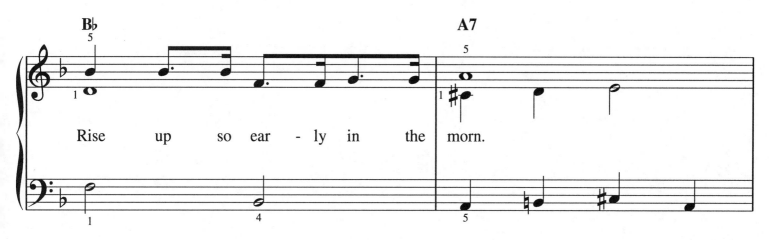

Rise up so ear - ly in the morn.

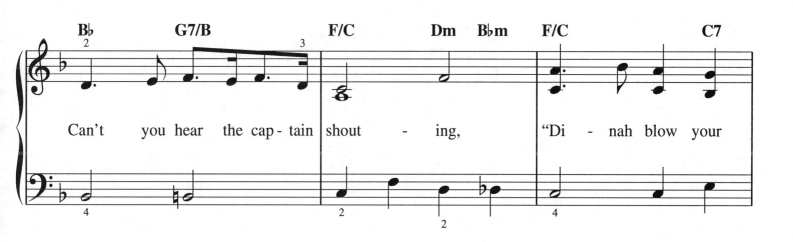

Can't you hear the cap - tain shout - ing, "Di - nah blow your

horn!" Di - nah won't you blow, Di - nah won't you blow,

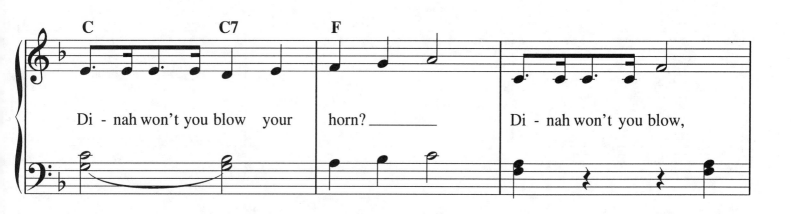

Di - nah won't you blow your horn?_____ Di - nah won't you blow,

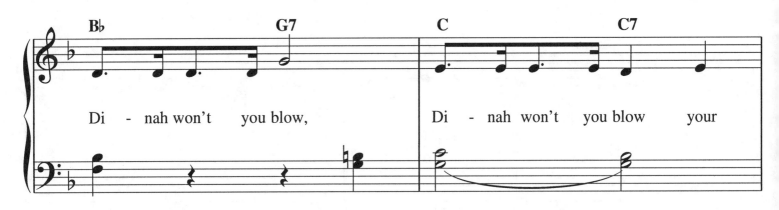

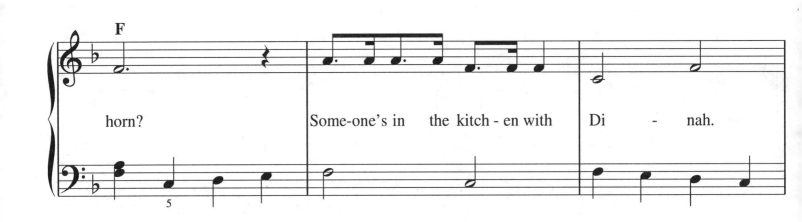

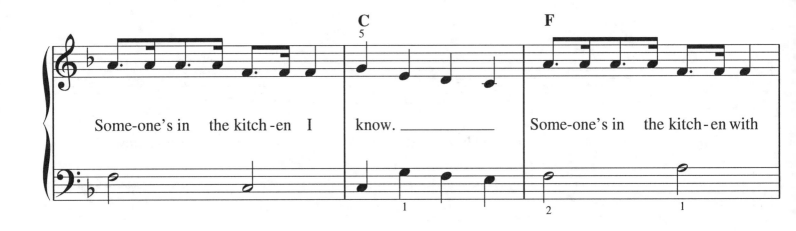

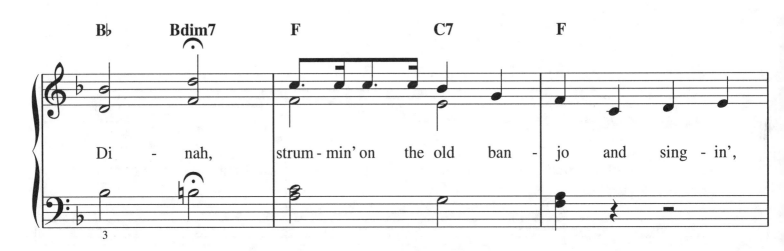

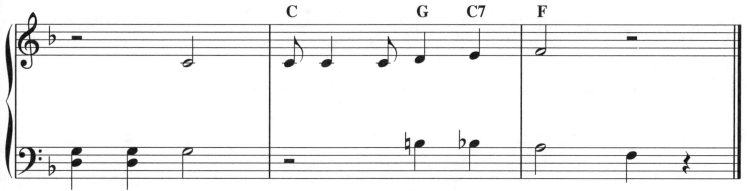

IF YOU'RE HAPPY
(And You Know It)

IT'S RAINING, IT'S POURING

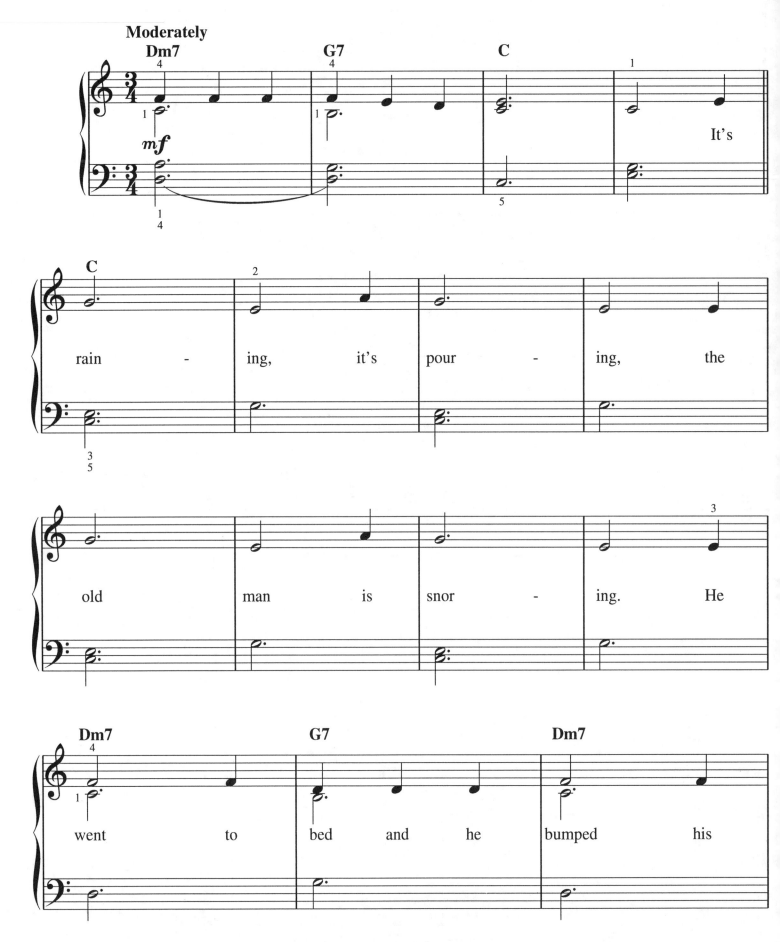

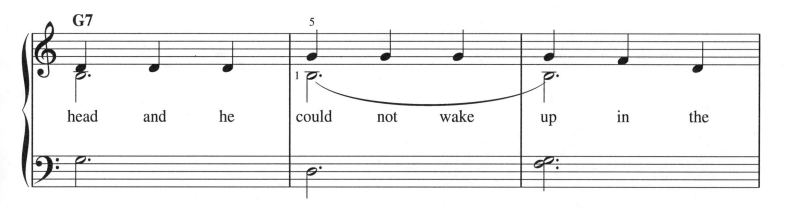

head   and   he   could   not   wake   up   in   the

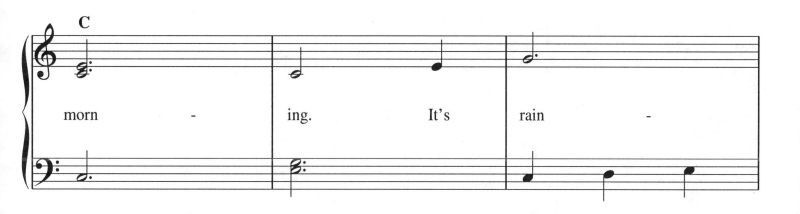

morn   -   ing.   It's   rain   -

ing,   it's   pour   -   ing,   the

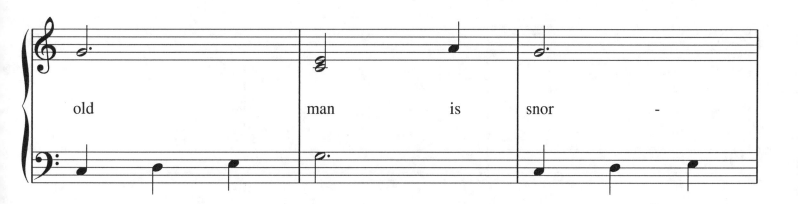

old   man   is   snor   -

ing.   He   went   to   bed   and   he

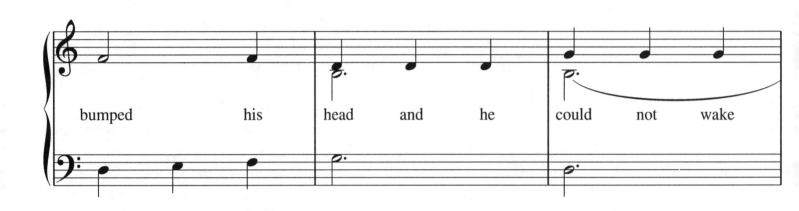

bumped   his   head   and   he   could   not   wake

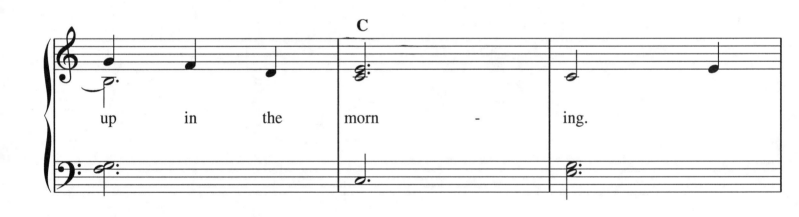

up   in   the   morn   -   ing.

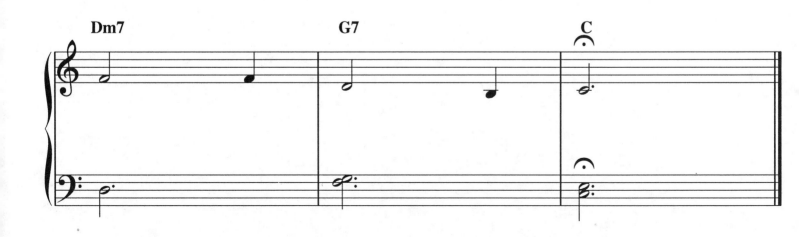

THE MARVELOUS TOY

Words and Music by
TOM PAXTON

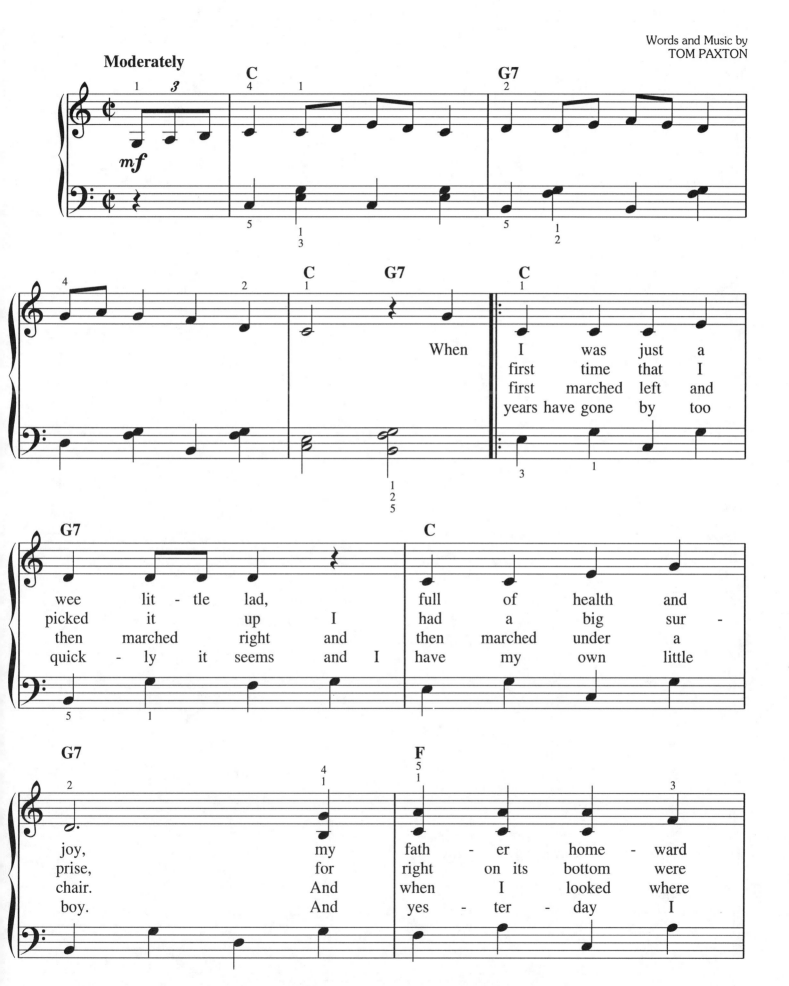

58

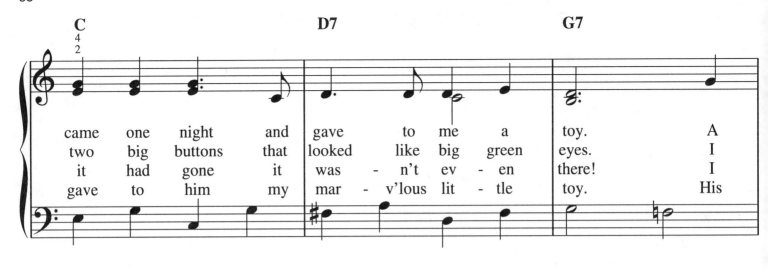

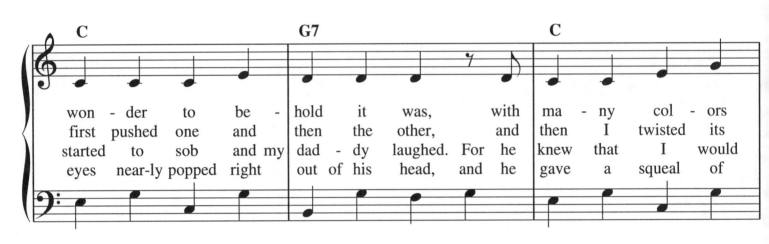

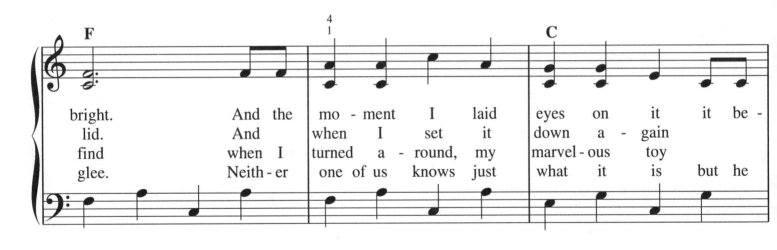

"Bop" when it stopped,   and "Whirr"   when it stood still. I
"Bop" when it stops,   and "Whirr"   when it stands still.

nev - er knew just   what it was and I   guess I   nev - er

1.-3.   4.

will   will.
     The
     It
     Well, the

JACK AND JILL

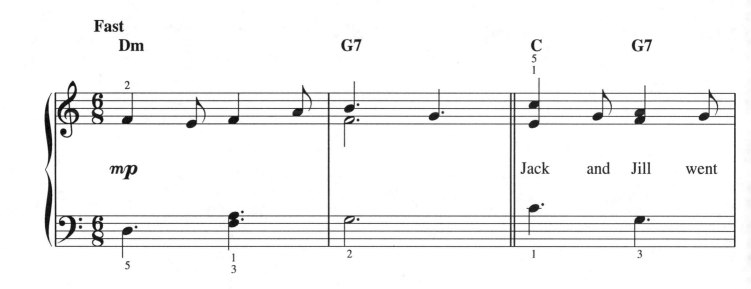

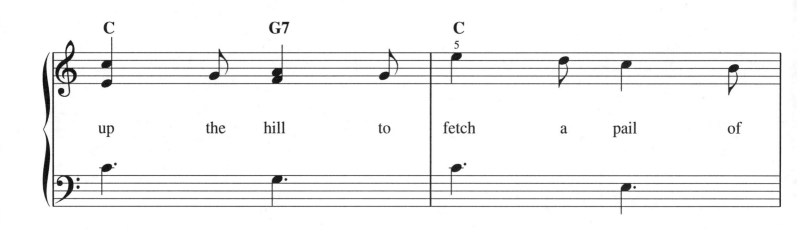

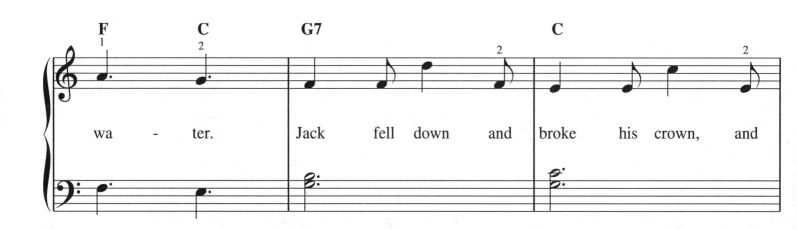

61

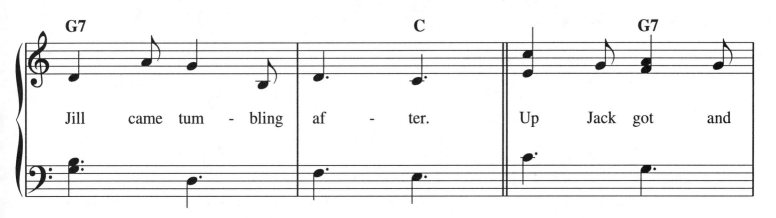

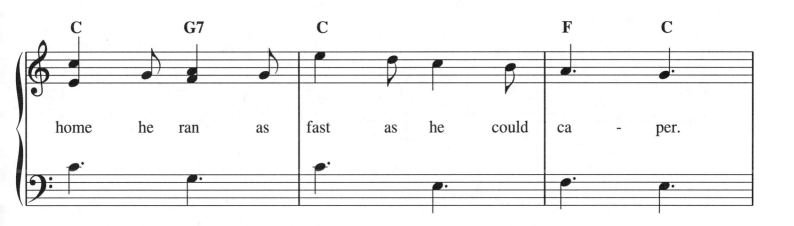

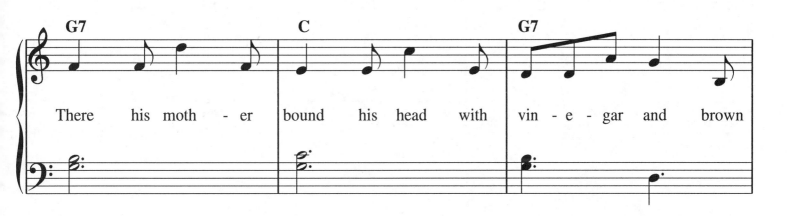

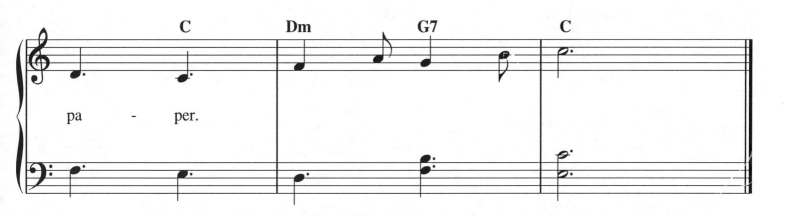

LAZY MARY, WILL YOU GET UP

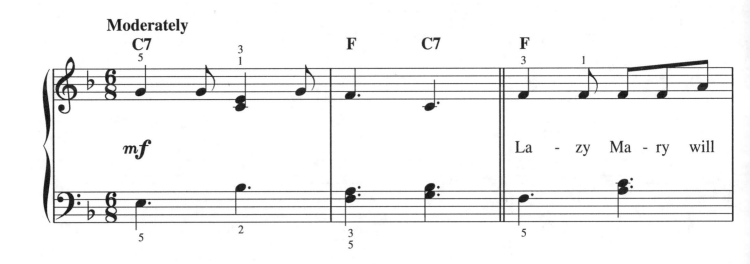

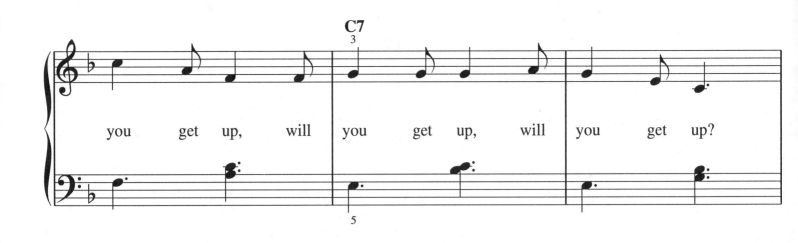

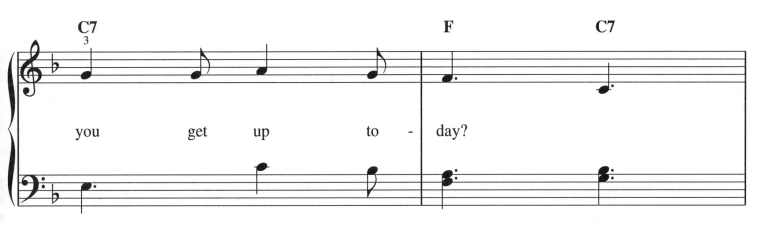

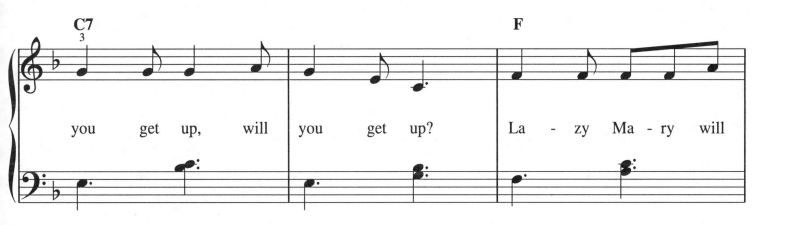

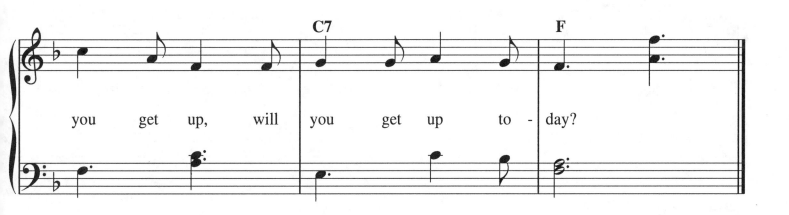

LITTLE BO PEEP

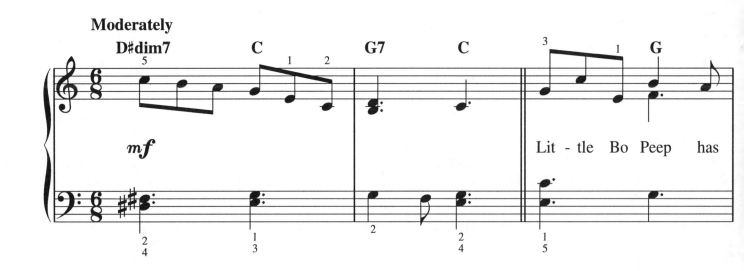

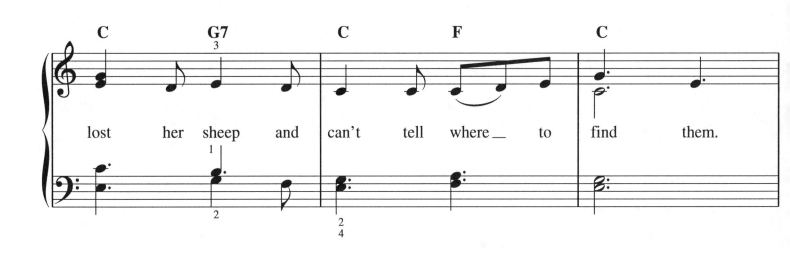

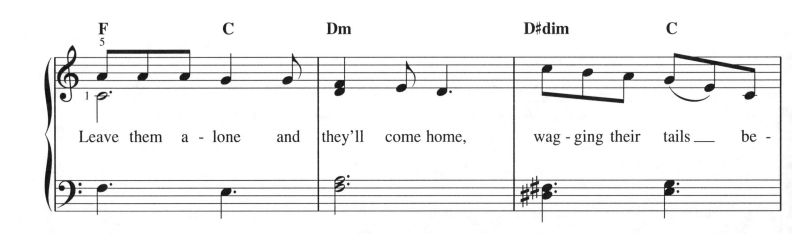

hind them. Lit - tle Bo Peep fell fast a - sleep and

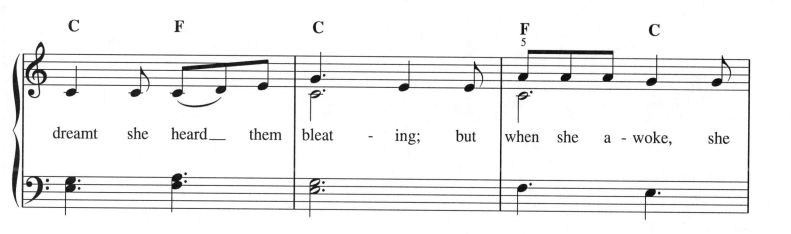

dreamt she heard___ them bleat - ing; but when she a - woke, she

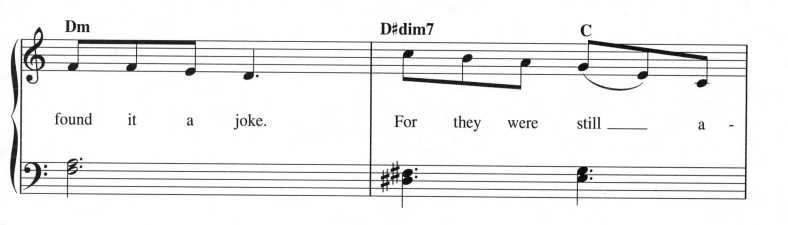

found it a joke. For they were still _____ a -

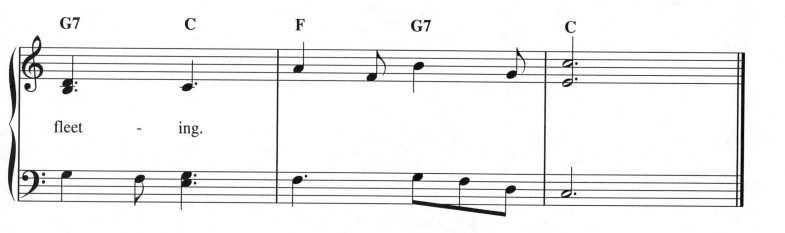

fleet - ing.

LONDON BRIDGE

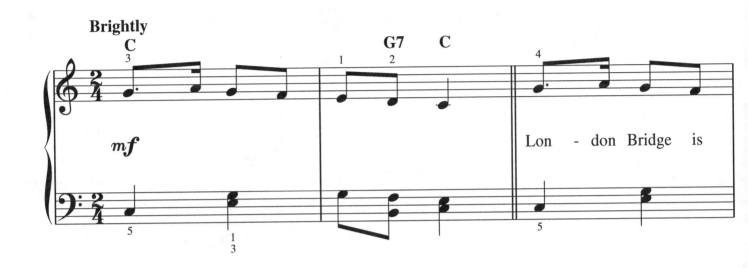

MARY HAD A LITTLE LAMB

G7 **C** **G7** **C**

fleece was white as snow. Ev - 'ry-where that
was a - gainst the rules. It made the child - ren

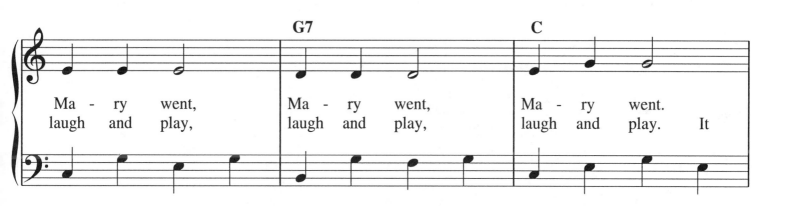

G7 **C**

Ma - ry went, Ma - ry went, Ma - ry went.
laugh and play, laugh and play, laugh and play. It

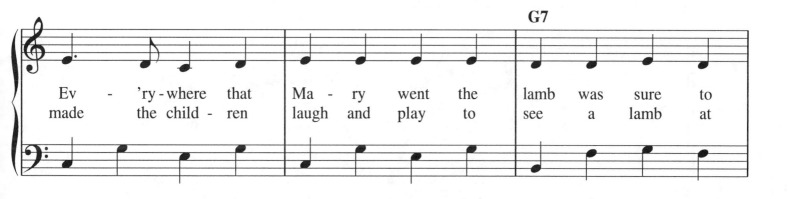

G7

Ev - 'ry-where that Ma - ry went the lamb was sure to
made the child - ren laugh and play to see a lamb at

1. **C**

2. **G7** **C**

go. It school.

THE MULBERRY BUSH

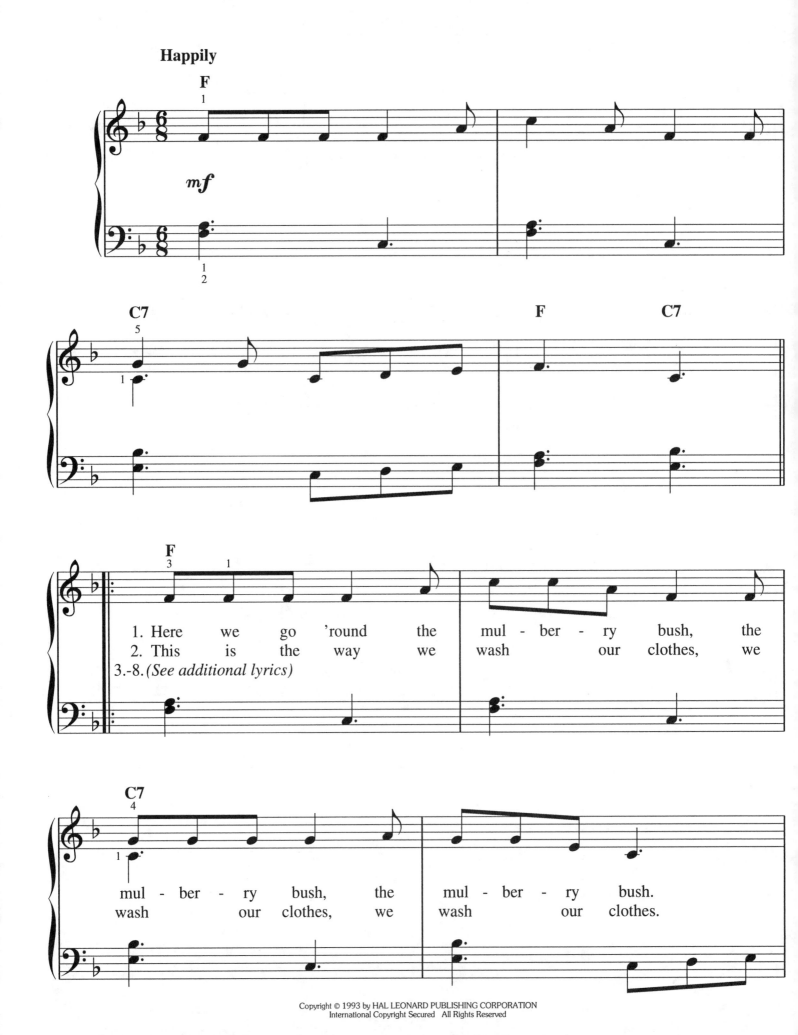

1. Here we go 'round the mul - ber - ry bush, the
2. This is the way we wash our clothes, we

3.-8. *(See additional lyrics)*

mul - ber - ry bush, the mul - ber - ry bush.
wash our clothes, we wash our clothes.

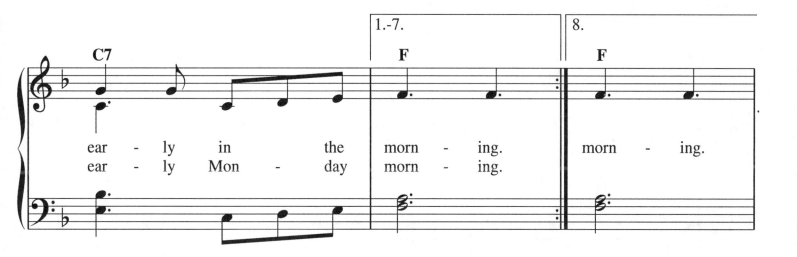

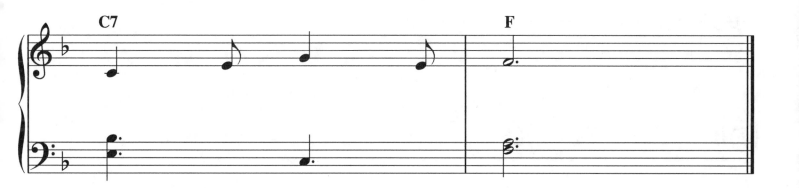

Additional Lyrics

3. This is the way we iron our clothes, etc.
So early Tuesday morning.

4. This is the way we scrub the floor, etc.
So early Wednesday morning.

5. This is the way we mend our clothes, etc.
So early Thursday morning.

6. This is the way we sweep the house, etc.
So early Friday morning.

7. This is the way we bake our bread, etc.
So early Saturday morning.

8. This is the way we go to church, etc.
So early Sunday morning.

MY FAVORITE THINGS
(From "THE SOUND OF MUSIC")

Lyrics by OSCAR HAMMERSTEIN II
Music by RICHARD RODGERS

Lively, in one (♩. = 1 beat)

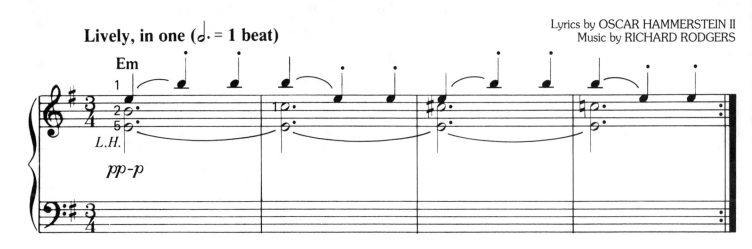

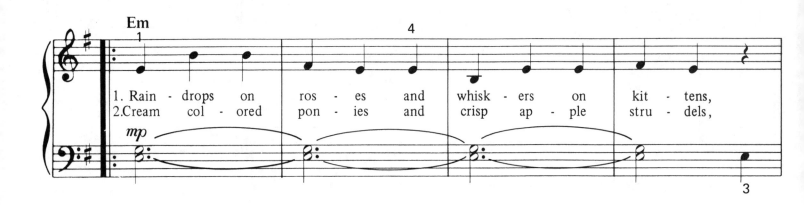

1. Rain - drops on ros - es and whisk - ers on kit - tens,
2. Cream col - ored pon - ies and crisp ap - ple stru - dels,

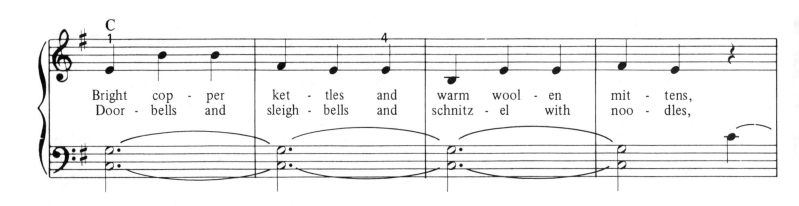

Bright cop - per ket - tles and warm wool - en mit - tens,
Door - bells and sleigh - bells and schnitz - el with noo - dles,

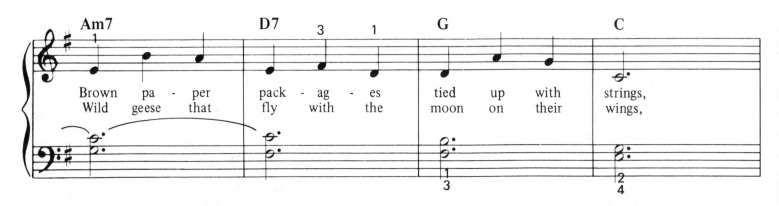

Brown pa - per pack - ag - es tied up with strings,
Wild geese that fly with the moon on their wings,

These are a few of my fav - or - ite things.
These are a few of my fav - or - ite things.

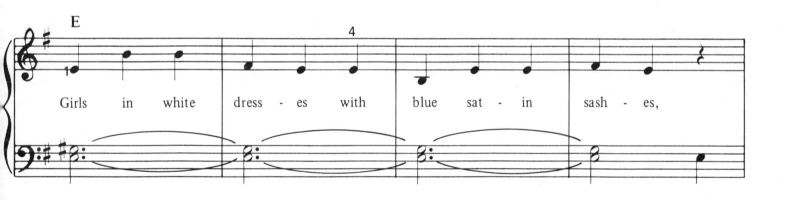

Girls in white dress - es with blue sat - in sash - es,

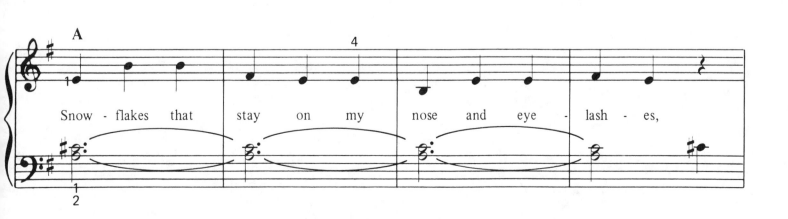

Snow - flakes that stay on my nose and eye - lash - es,

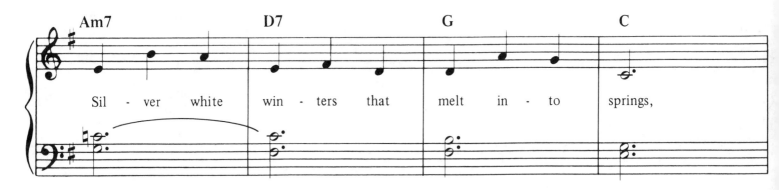

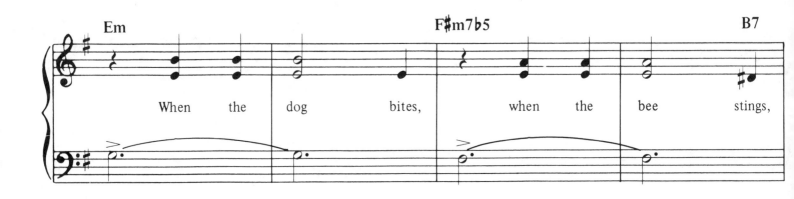

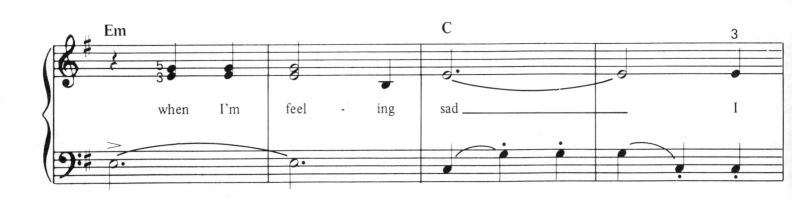

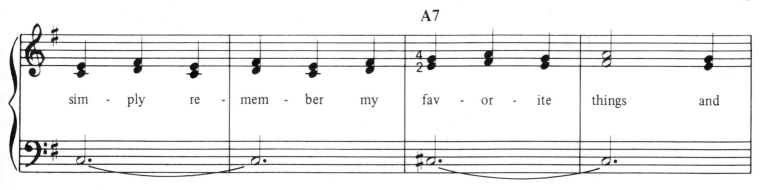

simp - ply re - mem - ber my fav - or - ite things and

then I don't feel so

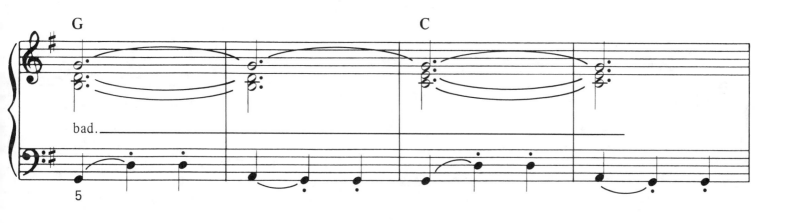

bad.

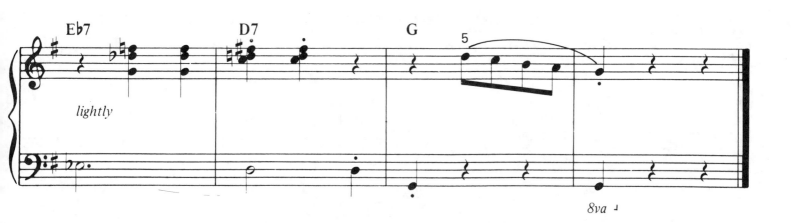

lightly

8va

OH WHERE, OH WHERE HAS MY LITTLE DOG GONE

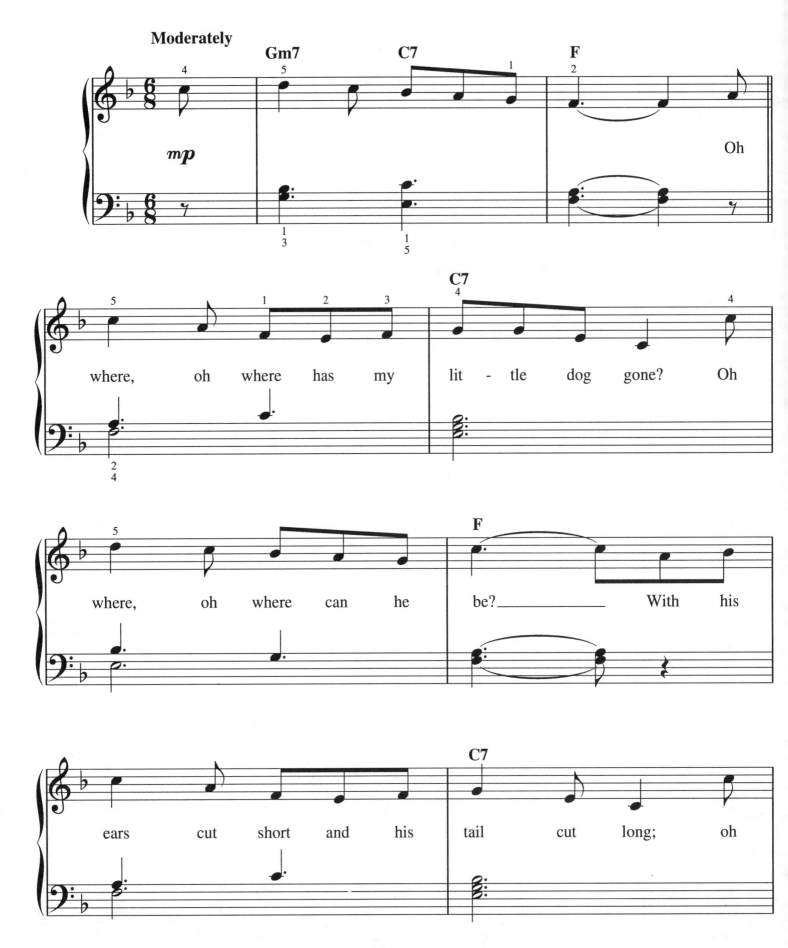

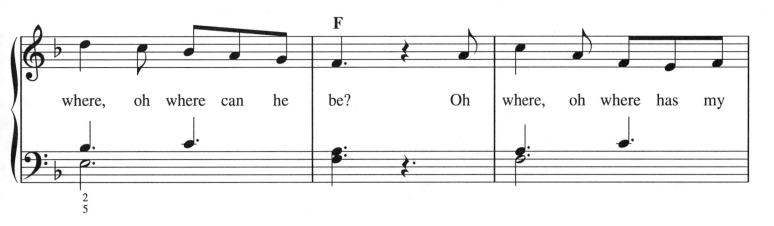

where, oh where can he be? Oh where, oh where has my

lit – tle dog gone? Oh where, oh where can he

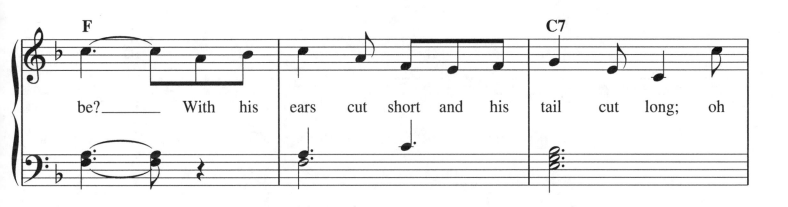

be?_____ With his ears cut short and his tail cut long; oh

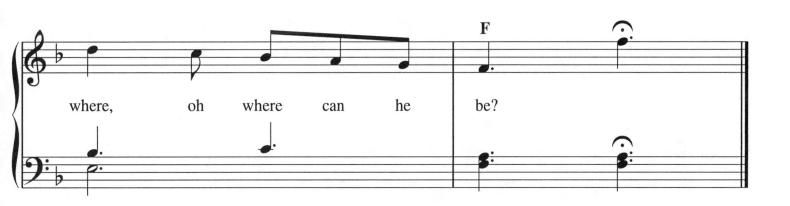

where, oh where can he be?

OLD KING COLE

Old King Cole was a mer-ry old soul, and a mer-ry old soul was

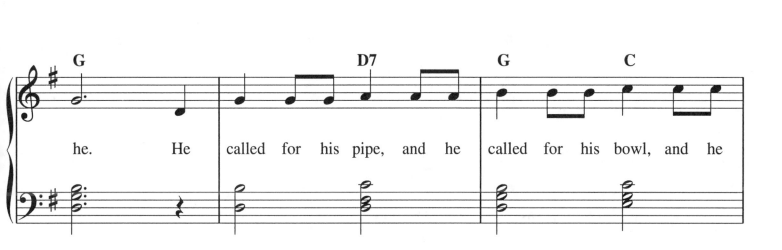

he. He called for his pipe, and he called for his bowl, and he

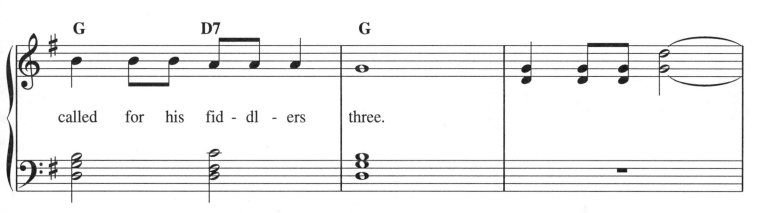

called for his fid-dl-ers three.

OLD MACDONALD HAD A FARM

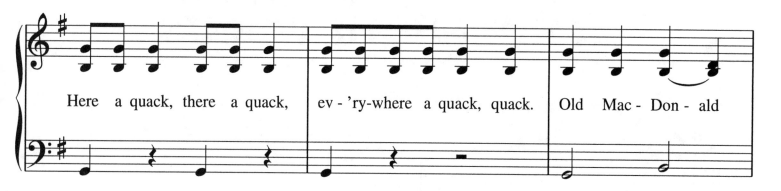

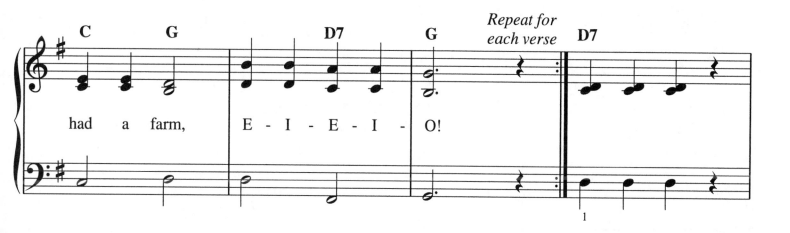

Additional Lyrics

2. Old MacDonald Had a Farm,
E - I - E - I - O!
And on this farm he had a chick,
E - I - E - I - O!
With a chick, chick here
And a chick, chick there,
Here a chick, there a chick,
Everywhere a chick, chick
Old MacDonald Had a Farm,
E - I - E - I - O!

3. Other verses:

    3. Cow - moo, moo
    4. Dogs - bow, bow
    5. Pigs - oink, oink
    6. Rooster - cock-a-doodle, cock-a-doodle
    7. Turkey - gobble, gobble
    8. Cat - meow, meow
    9. Horse - neigh, neigh
  10. Donkey - hee-haw, hee-haw

OVER THE RIVER AND THROUGH THE WOODS

OH, SUSANNA

Moderately

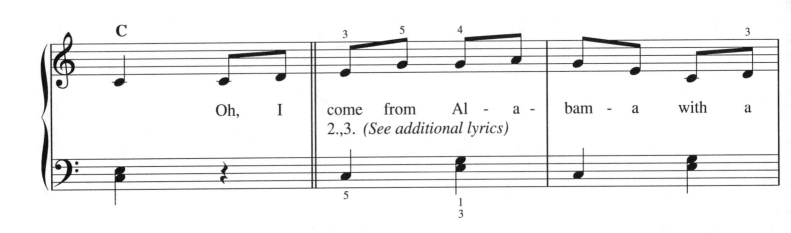

Oh, I come from Al - a - bam - a with a
2.,3. *(See additional lyrics)*

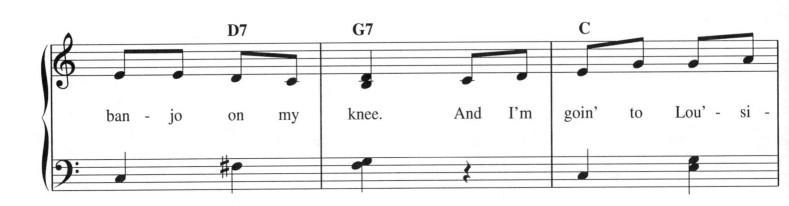

ban - jo on my knee. And I'm goin' to Lou' - si -

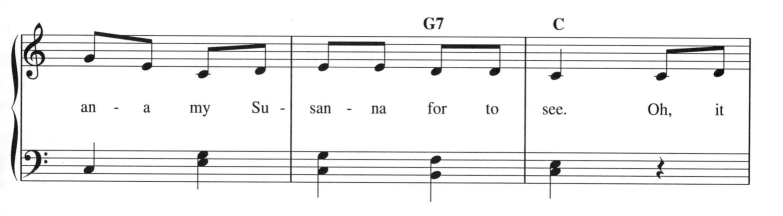

an - a my Su - san - na for to see. Oh, it

rained all night the day I left, the weath - er it was

dry. The_____ sun so hot I froze to death. Su -

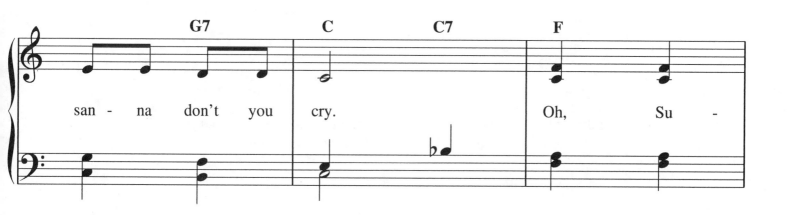

san - na don't you cry. Oh, Su -

san - na,   oh   don't   you   cry   for   me,   for   I

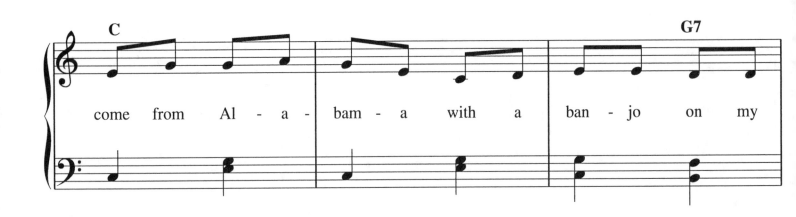

come   from   Al - a - bam - a   with   a   ban - jo   on   my

knee.

Additional Lyrics

2. I had a dream the other night
   When everything was still.
   I thought I saw Susanna
   A-coming down the hill.

3. The buckwheat cake was in her mouth,
   The tear was in her eye,
   Say I, "I'm coming from the South,
   Susanna, don't you cry."

POLLY WOLLY DOODLE

Bright, with humor

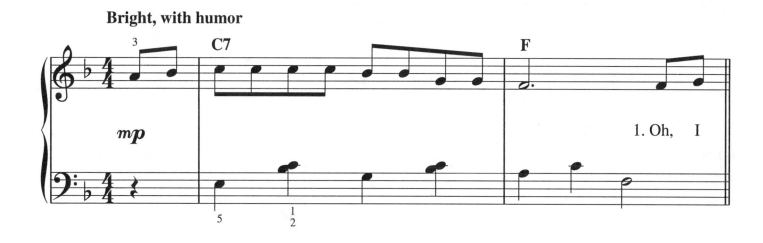

1. Oh, I

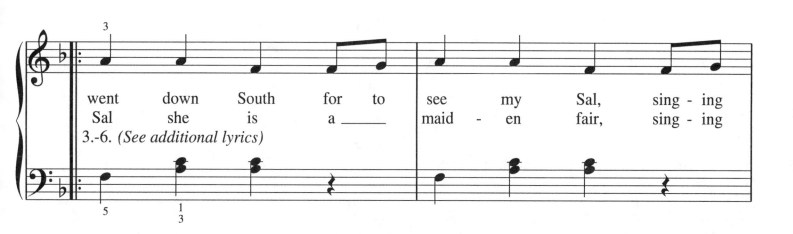

went   down   South   for   to   see   my   Sal,   sing - ing
Sal   she   is   a _____   maid - en   fair,   sing - ing
3.-6. *(See additional lyrics)*

Pol - ly   Wol - ly   Doo - dle   all   the   day.   My _____
Pol - ly   Wol - ly   Doo - dle   all   the   day.   With _____

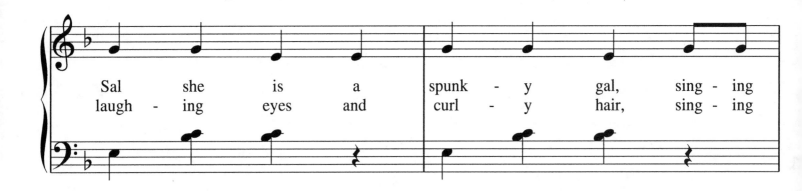

Sal she is a spunk - y gal, sing - ing
laugh - ing eyes and curl - y hair, sing - ing

Pol - ly Wol - ly Doo - dle all the day.
Pol - ly Wol - ly Doo - dle all the day.

F   Chorus

Fare thee

well, fare thee well. Fare thee well, my fair - y

C7

fay. For I'm goin' to Lou' - si - an - a for to

see my Su - zi - an - na, sing - ing Pol - ly Wol - ly Doo - dle all the

1.-5. **F**

day.

2. Oh, my
3. Oh, a

6. **F**

day.

C7

F

Additional Lyrics

3. Oh, a grasshopper sittin' on a railroad track,
   Singing Polly-Wolly Doodle all the day.
   A pickin' his teeth with a carpet tack,
   Singing Polly-Wolly Doodle all the day.
   To Chorus:

4. Oh, I went to bed, but it wasn't no use,
   Singing Polly-Wolly Doodle all the day.
   My feet stuck out like a chicken roost,
   Singing Polly-Wolly Doodle all the day.
   To Chorus:

5. Behind the barn down on my knees,
   Singing Polly-Wolly Doodle all the day.
   I thought I heard a chicken sneeze,
   Singing Polly-Wolly Doodle all the day.
   To Chorus:

6. He sneezed so hard with the whooping cough,
   Singing Polly-Wolly Doodle all the day.
   He sneezed his head and tail right off,
   Singing Polly-Wolly Doodle all the day.
   To Chorus:

POP! GOES THE WEASEL

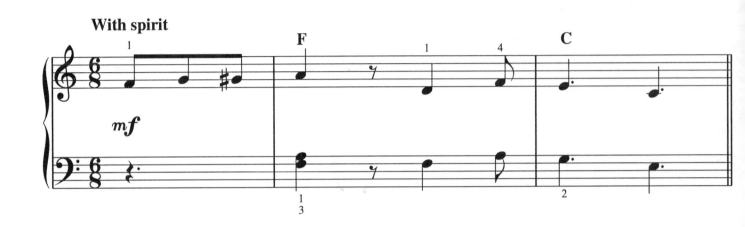

All a-round the cob-ler's bench the mon-key chased the
Ru-fus has the whoop-ing cough, and Sal-ly has the

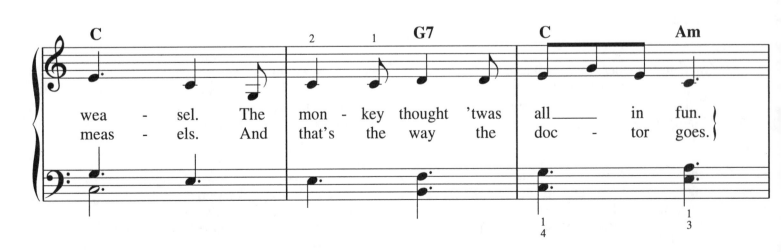

wea-sel. The mon-key thought 'twas all_____ in fun.
meas-els. And that's the way the doc-tor goes.

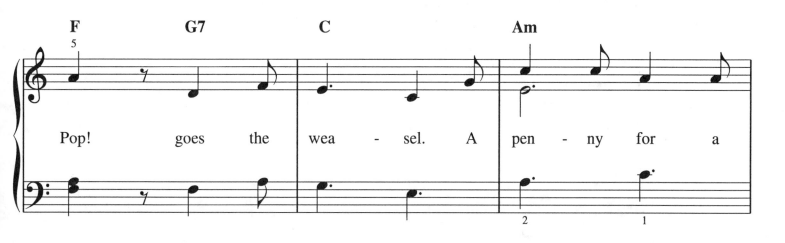

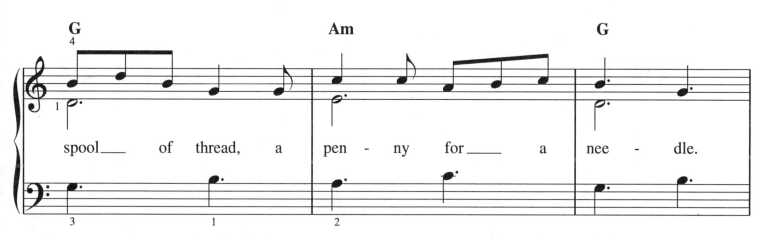

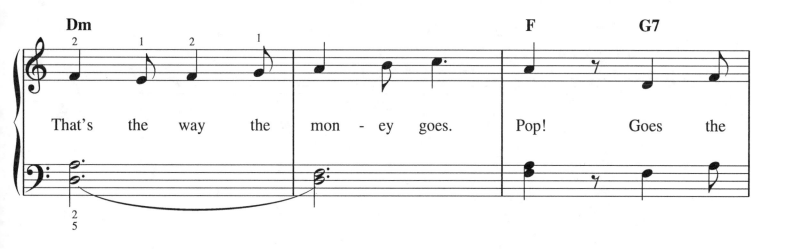

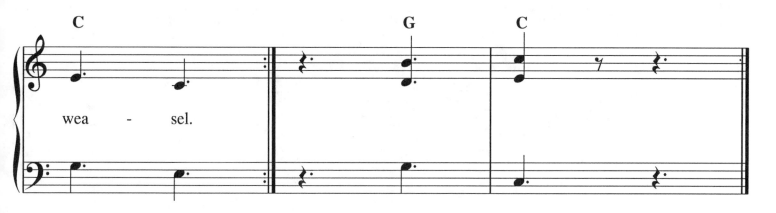

THE RAINBOW CONNECTION
(From "THE MUPPET MOVIE")

By PAUL WILLIAMS
and KENNETH L. ASCHER

with pedal

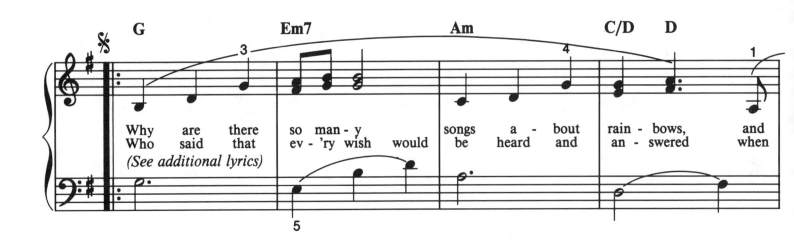

Why are there so man-y songs a-bout rain-bows, and
Who said that ev-'ry wish would be heard and an-swered when
(See additional lyrics)

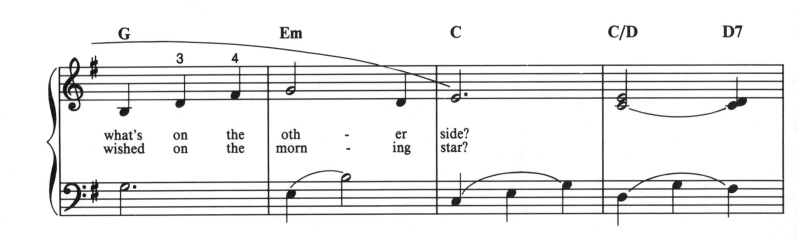

what's on the oth - er side?
wished on the morn - ing star?

Rain - bows are vi - sions, __ but on - ly il - lu - sions, And
Some - bod - y thought of that, and some - one be - lieved it;

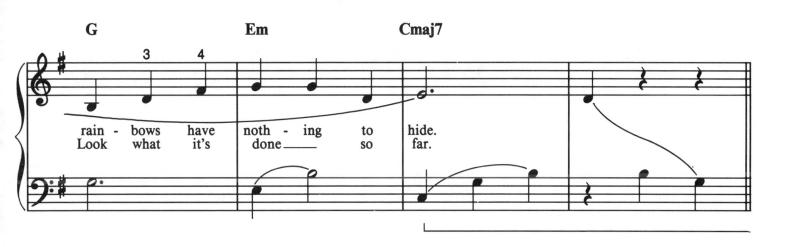

rain - bows have noth - ing to hide.
Look what it's done __ so far.

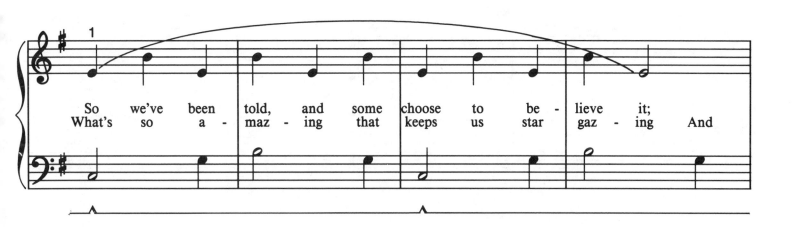

So we've been told, and some choose to be - lieve it;
What's so a - maz - ing that keeps us star - gaz - ing And

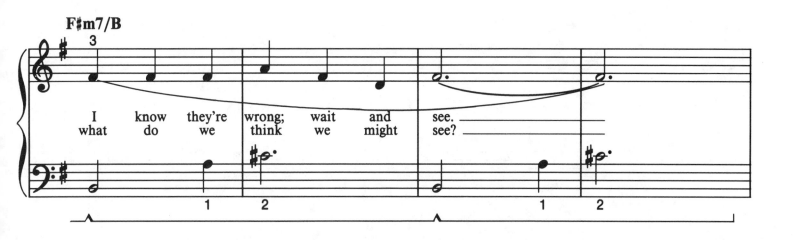

I know they're wrong; wait and see. __
what do we think we and might see? __

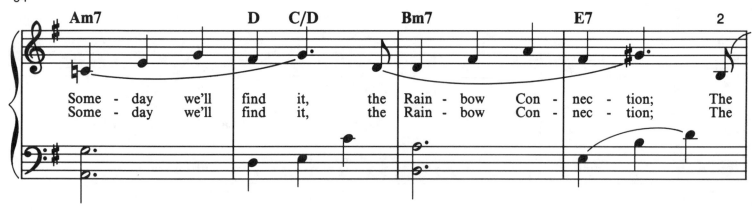

Some - day we'll find it, the Rain - bow Con - nec - tion; The
Some - day we'll find it, the Rain - bow Con - nec - tion; The

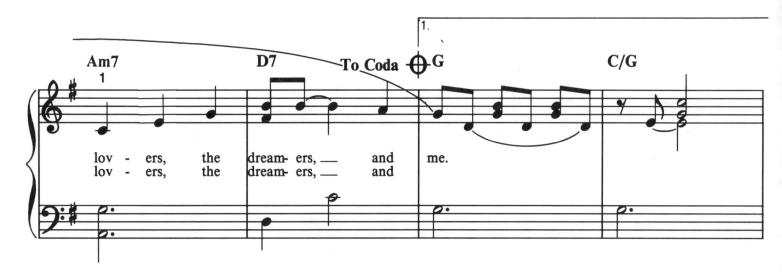

lov - ers, the dream- ers, ___ and me.
lov - ers, the dream- ers, ___ and

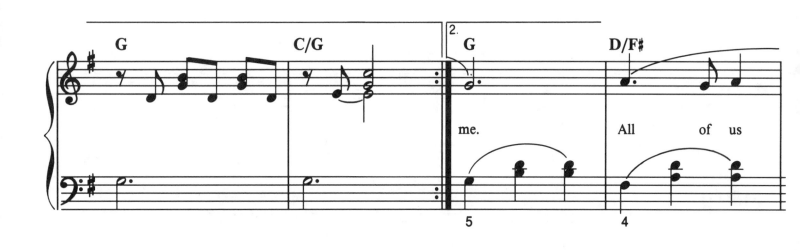

me. All of us

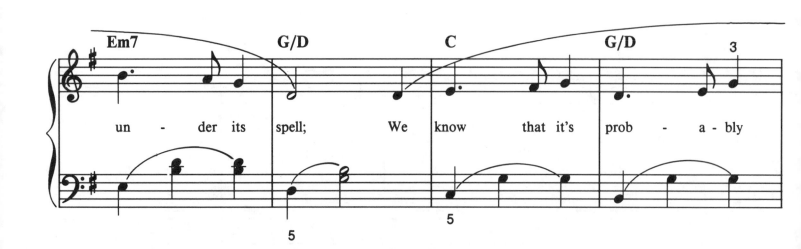

un - der its spell; We know that it's prob - a - bly

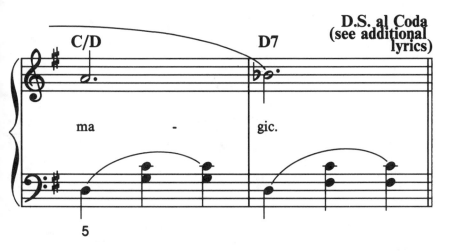

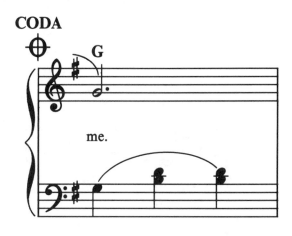

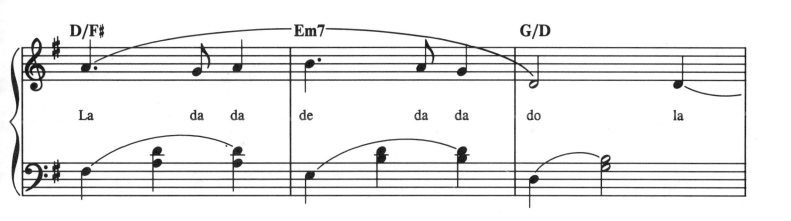

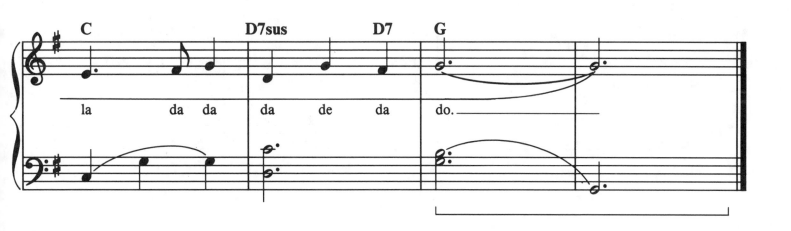

Additional Lyrics

Verse 3: Have you been half asleep and have you heard voices?
I've heard them calling my name.
Is this the sweet sound that calls the young sailors?
The voice might be one and the same.
I've heard it too many times to ignore it.
It's something that I'm s'posed to be.
Someday we'll find it,
The Rainbow Connection;
The lovers, the dreamers and (me.)
(To Coda)

RING AROUND THE ROSIE

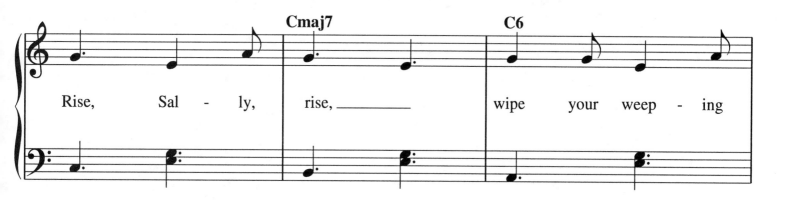

Rise, Sal - ly, rise, _____ wipe your weep - ing

eyes; _____ fly to the east,

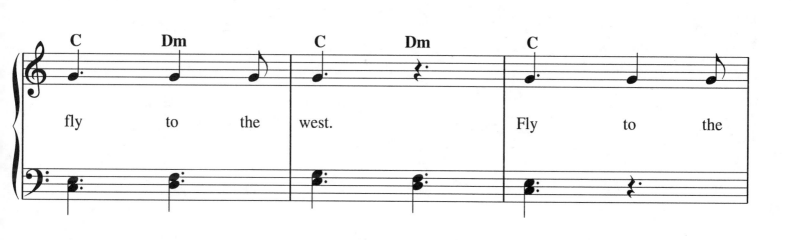

fly to the west. Fly to the

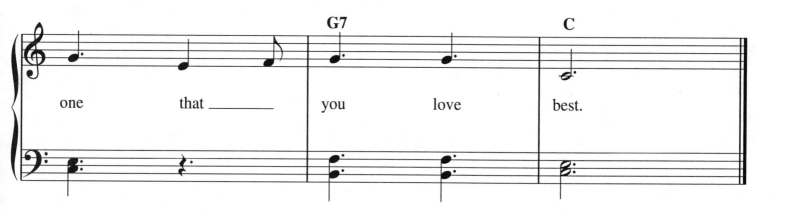

one that _____ you love best.

ROCK-A-BYE, BABY

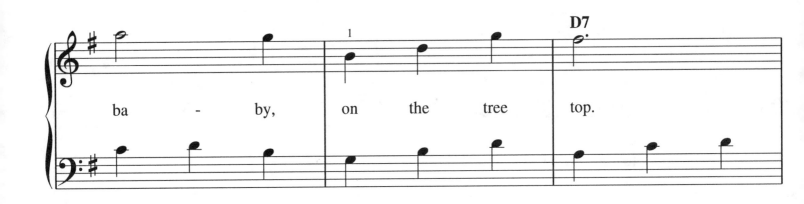

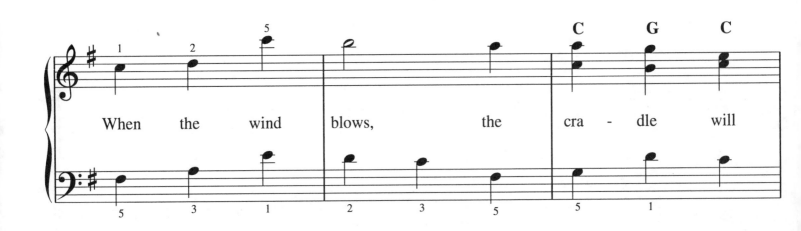

rock.   When   the   bough   breaks   the

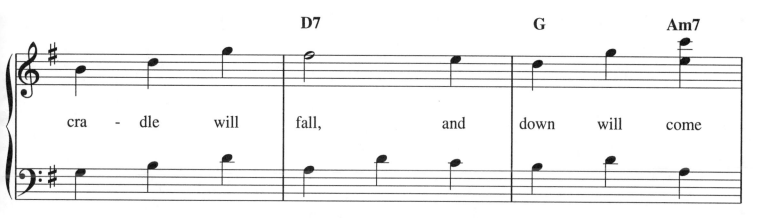

cra - dle   will   fall,   and   down   will   come

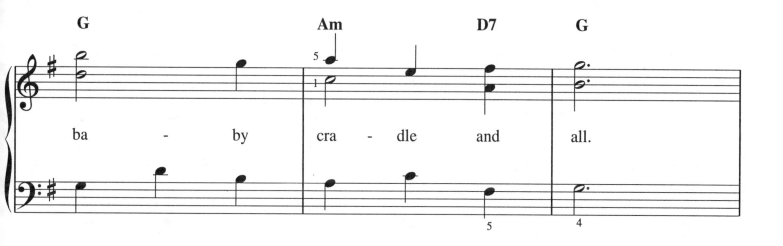

ba - by   cra - dle   and   all.

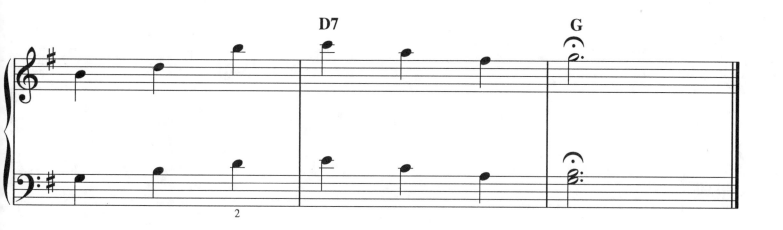

ROW, ROW, ROW YOUR BOAT

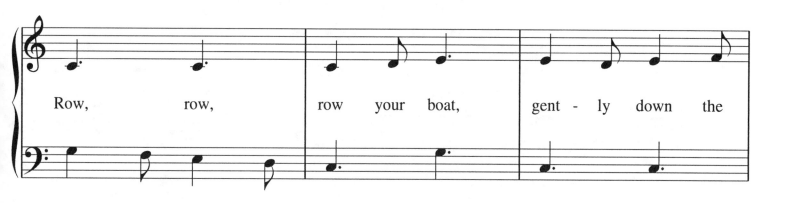

Row, row, row your boat, gent - ly down the

stream. Mer - ri - ly, mer - ri - ly,

mer - ri - ly, mer - ri - ly. Life is but a

dream.

RUBBER DUCKIE

Words and Music by
JEFFREY MOSS

Rub - ber Duck - ie, you're my ver - y best friend it's true.

Oh, ev - 'ry day when I make my way to the tub - by,

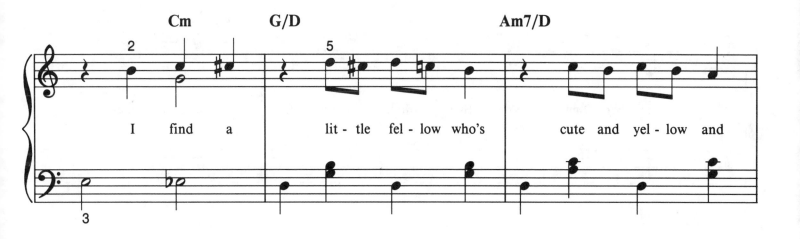

I find a lit - tle fel - low who's cute and yel - low and

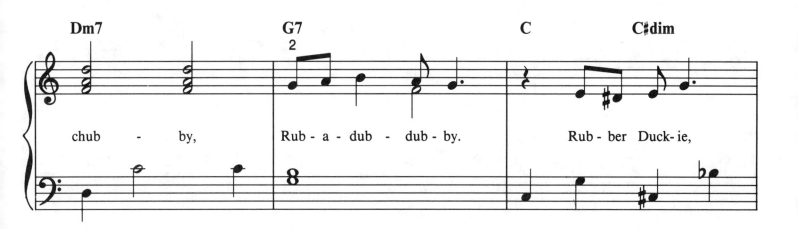

chub - by, Rub - a - dub - dub - by. Rub - ber Duck - ie,

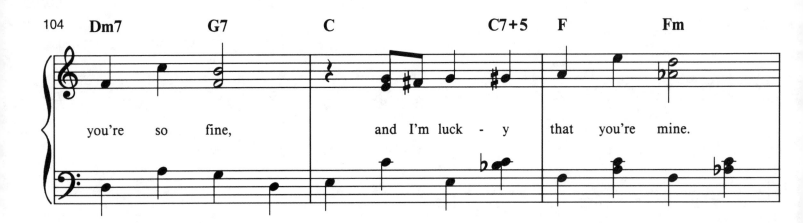

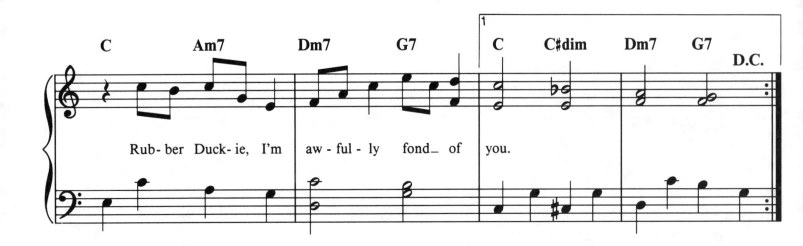

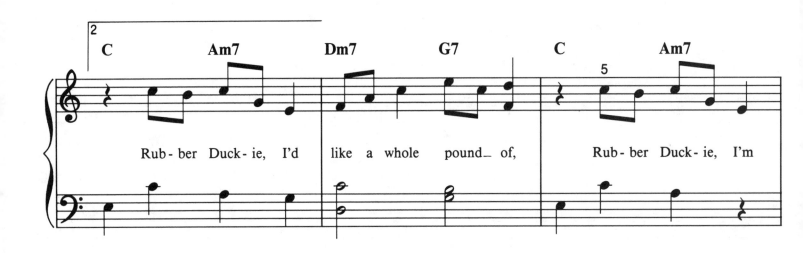

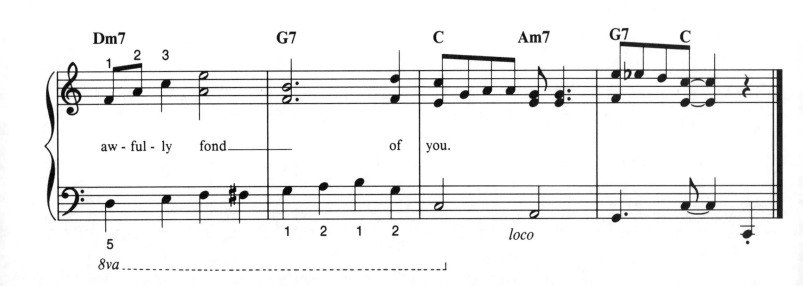

SING A SONG OF SIXPENCE

Moderately

birds be - gan to sing. Was - n't that a

dain - ty dish to set be - fore the king? The

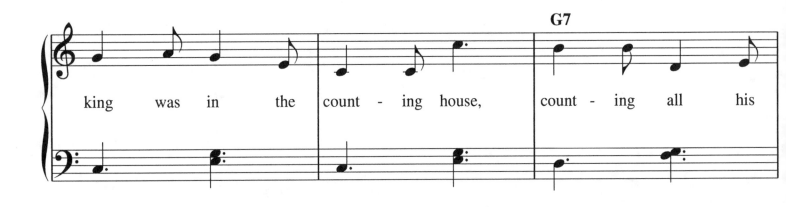

king was in the count - ing house, count - ing all his

mon - ey._____ The queen was in the par - lor,

eat - ing bread and hon - ey._____ The maid was in the

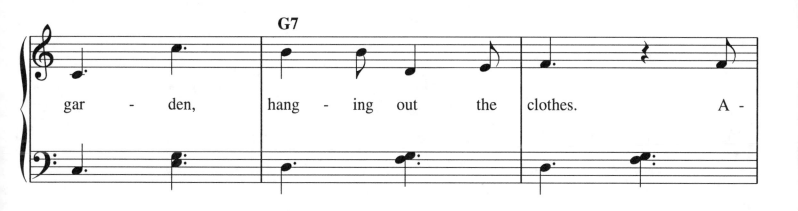

gar - den, hang - ing out the clothes. A -

long_____ came a black - bird and pecked ____ off her

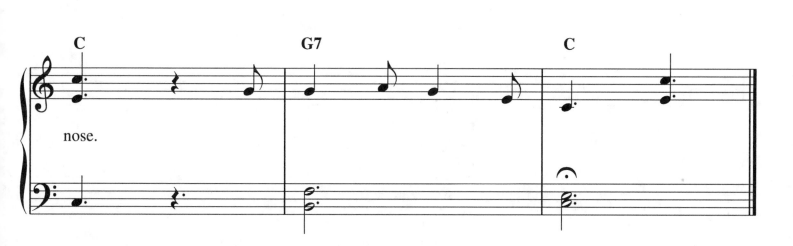

nose.

SING

Words and Music by
JOE RAPOSO

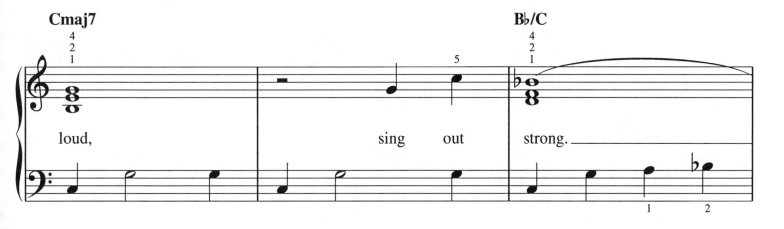

loud,   sing   out   strong. _____

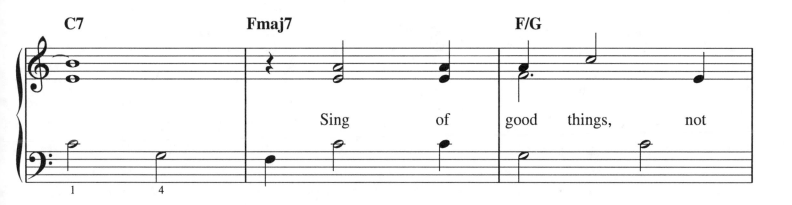

Sing   of   good   things,   not

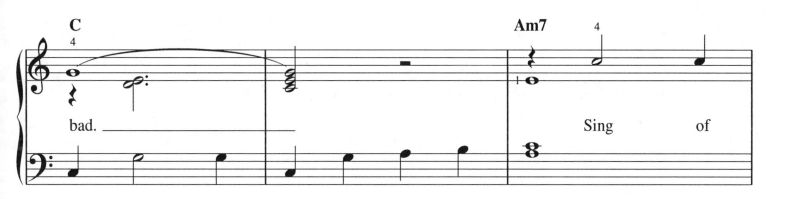

bad. _____   Sing   of

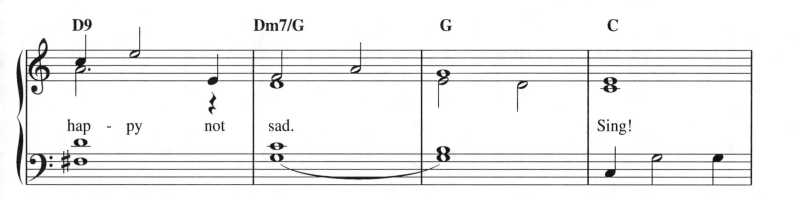

hap - py   not   sad.   Sing!

Sing a song. Make it sim - ple to

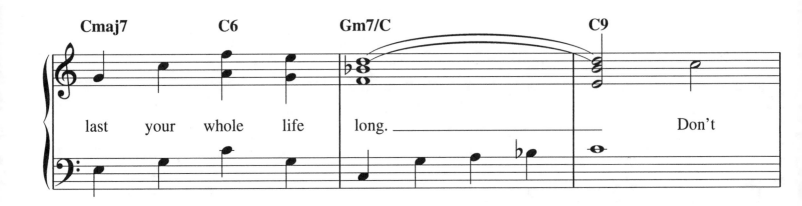

last your whole life long. _____ Don't

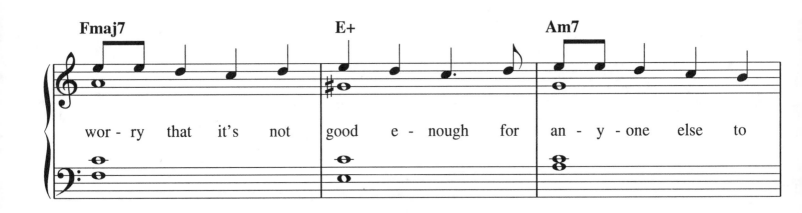

wor - ry that it's not good e - nough for an - y - one else to

hear. Sing! _____ Sing a song.

La la do la da, la

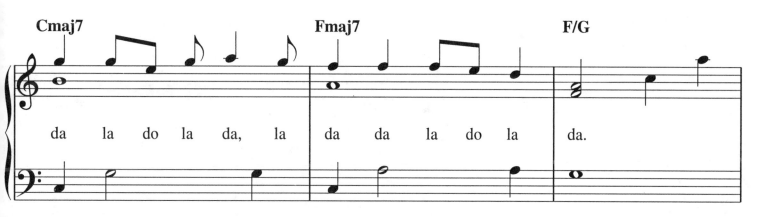

Cmaj7 da la do la da, la **Fmaj7** da da la do la **F/G** da.

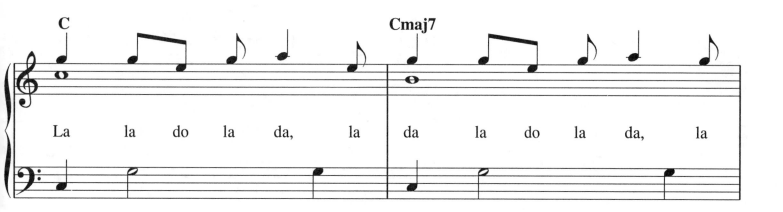

C La la do la da, la **Cmaj7** da la do la da, la

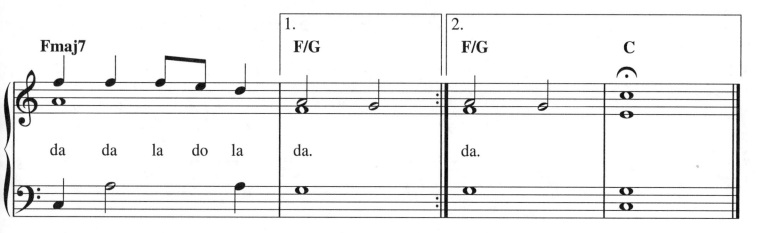

Fmaj7 da da la do la | **1.** **F/G** da. | **2.** **F/G** da. **C**

SKIP TO MY LOU

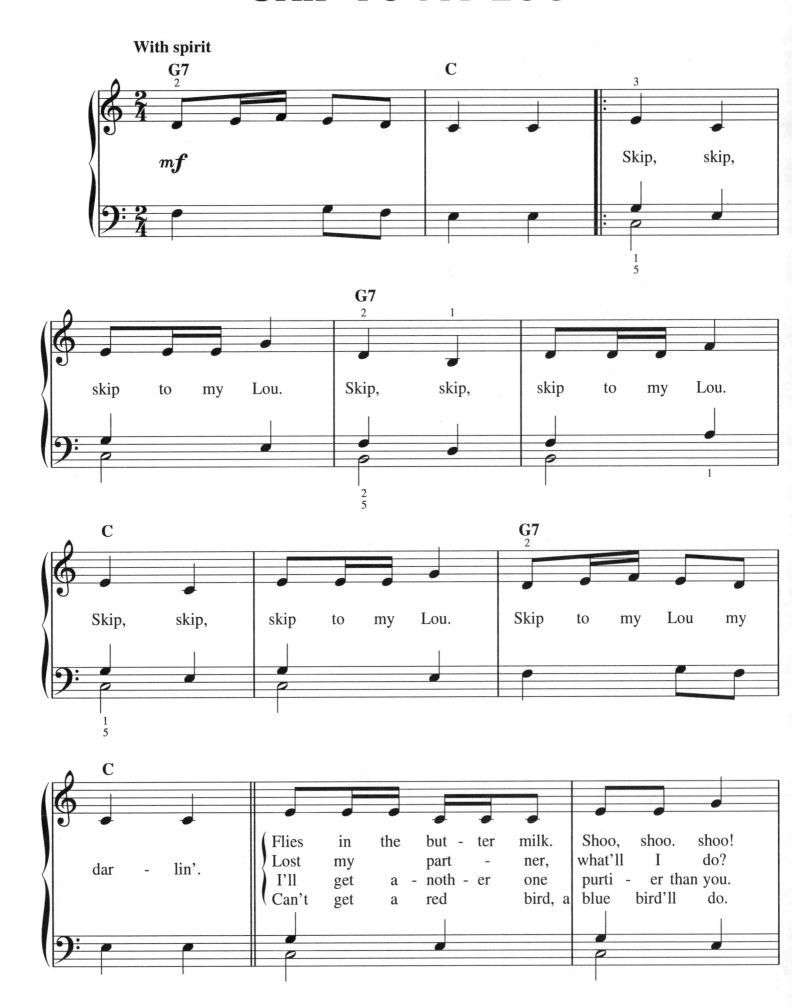

SOMEBODY COME AND PLAY

Words and Music by
JOE RAPOSO

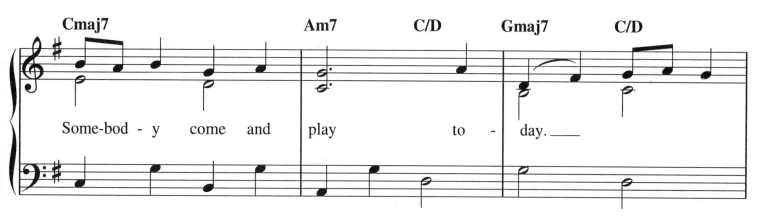

Some-bod - y come and play to - day. ____

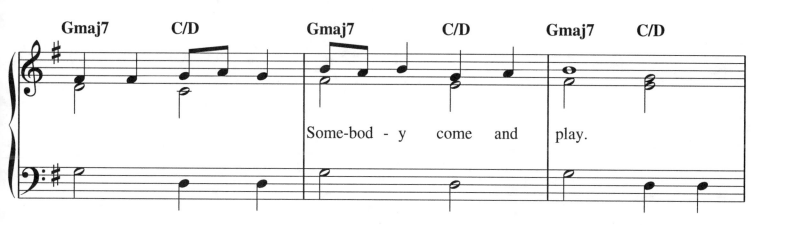

Some-bod - y come and play.

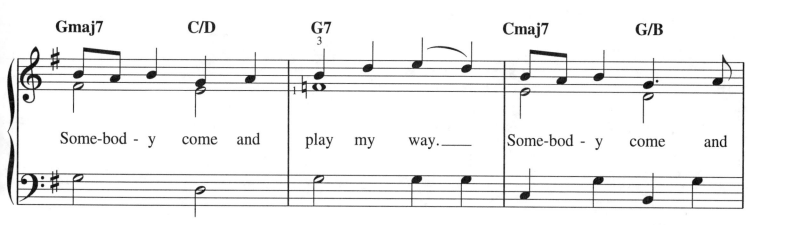

Some-bod - y come and play my way. ____ Some-bod - y come and

rhyme the rhymes and laugh the laughs. It won't take long.

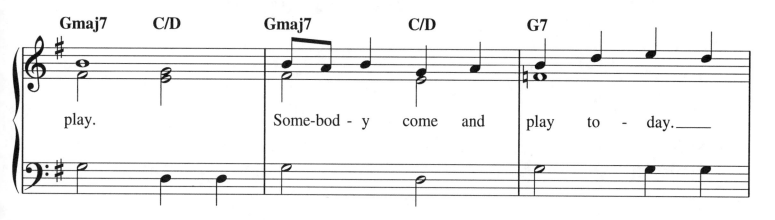

Gmaj7   C/D   Gmaj7   C/D   G7

play.   Some-bod - y come and   play to - day._____

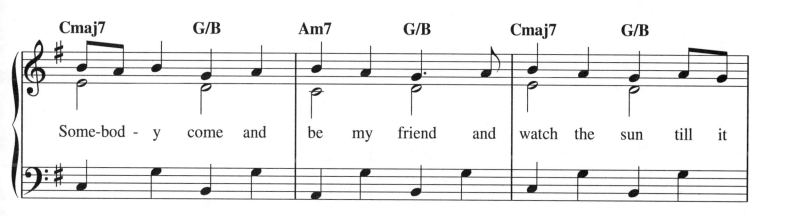

Cmaj7   G/B   Am7   G/B   Cmaj7   G/B

Some-bod - y come and   be my friend and   watch the sun till it

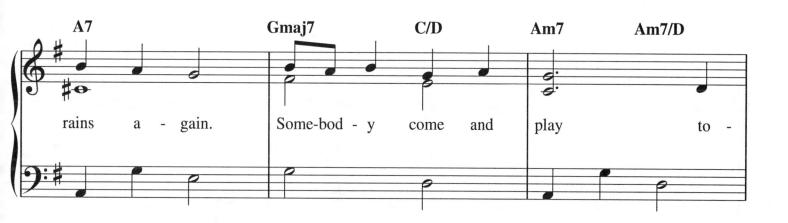

A7   Gmaj7   C/D   Am7   Am7/D

rains a - gain.   Some-bod - y come and   play   to -

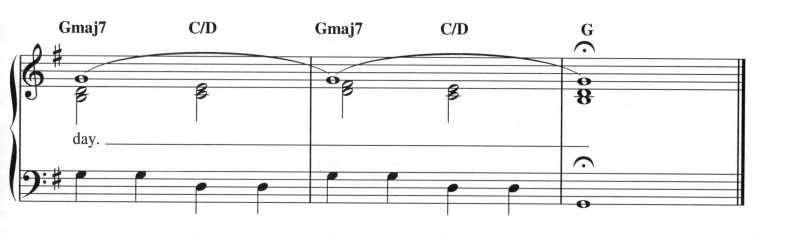

Gmaj7   C/D   Gmaj7   C/D   G

day._____

TEN LITTLE INDIANS

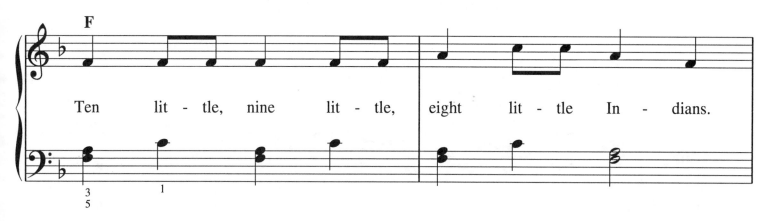

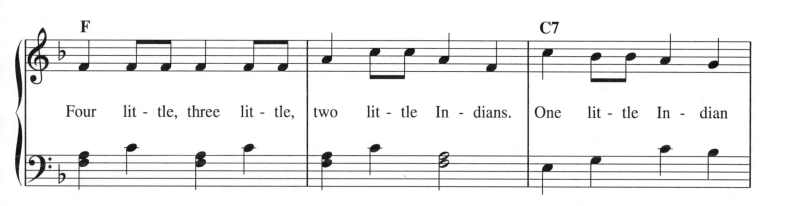

THIS OLD MAN

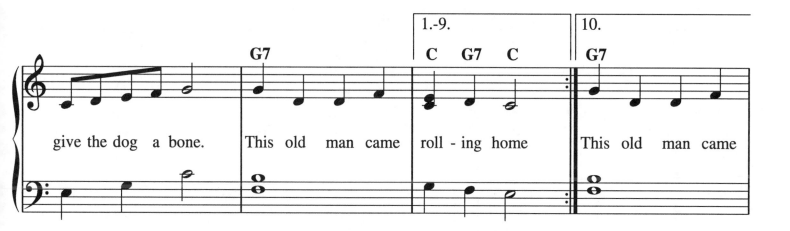

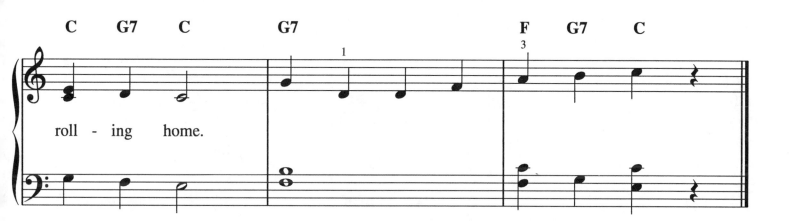

Additional Lyrics

3. This old man, he played three,
   He played knick-knack on my knee. *(Chorus)*

4. This old man, he played four,
   He played knick-knack on my door. *(Chorus)*

5. This old man, he played five,
   He played knick-knack on my hive. *(Chorus)*

6. This old man, he played six,
   He played knick-knack on my sticks. *(Chorus)*

7. This old man, he played seven,
   He played knick-knack up to heaven. *(Chorus)*

8. This old man, he played eight,
   He played knick-knack at the gate. *(Chorus)*

9. This old man, he played nine,
   He played knick-knack on my line. *(Chorus)*

10. This old man, he played ten,
    He played knick-knack over again. *(Chorus)*

THREE BLIND MICE

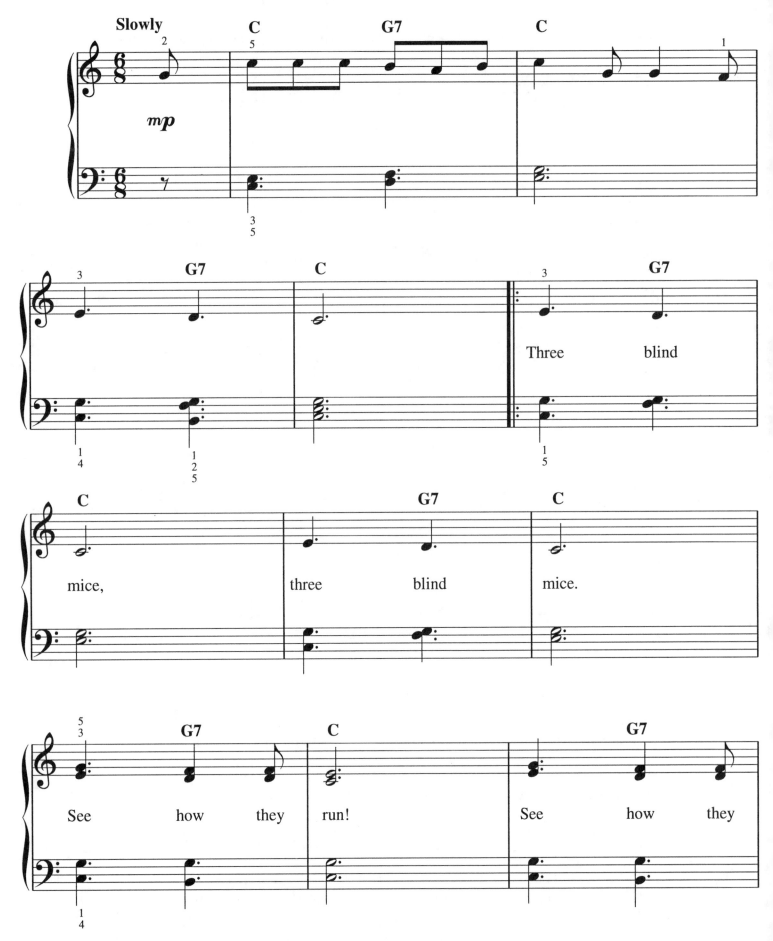

run! _____ They all ran af - ter the farm - er's wife, who

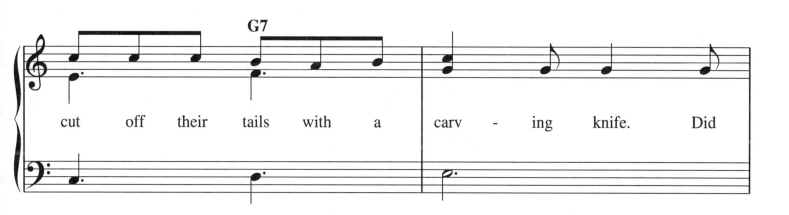

cut off their tails with a carv - ing knife. Did

you ev - er see such a sight in your life as three blind

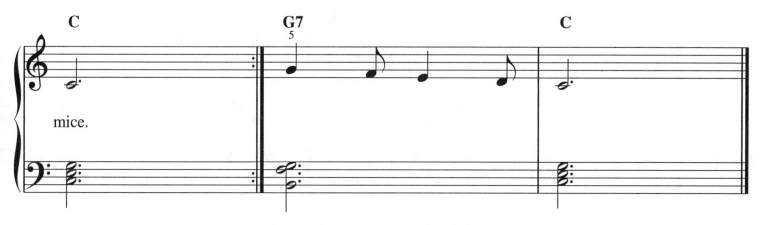

mice.

TWINKLE, TWINKLE, LITTLE STAR

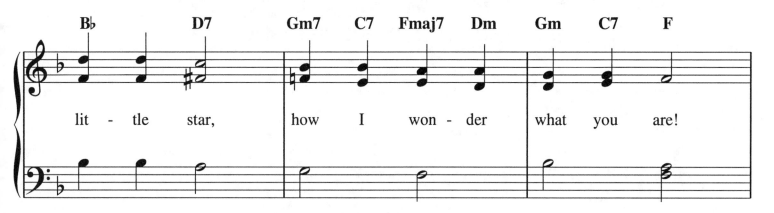

lit - tle star, how I won - der what you are!

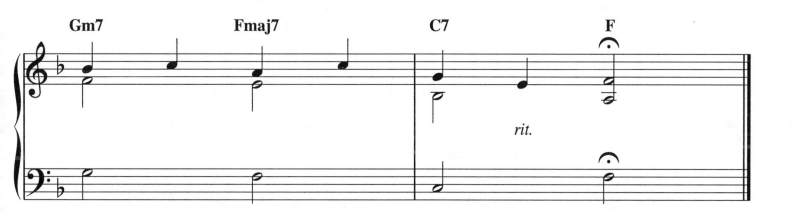

rit.

Additional Lyrics

THE ALPHABET SONG

A B C D E F G,
H I J K LMNOP,
Q R S, T U V,
W, X, Y, and Z.
Now you know my ABCs;
next time won't you sing with me?

BAA, BAA, BLACK SHEEP

Baa, baa, black sheep;
have you any wool?
"Yes, sir; yes sir.
Three bags full.
One for my master,
one for my dame,
one for the little boy
who lies in the lane."

Baa, baa, black sheep;
have you any wool?
"Yes, sir; yes sir.
Three bags full.

WON'T YOU BE MY NEIGHBOR?

(From "MR. ROGERS' NEIGHBORHOOD")

Words and Music by
FRED ROGERS

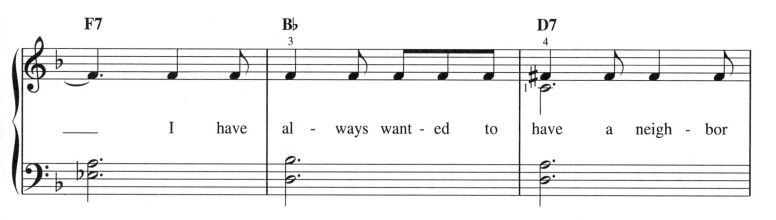

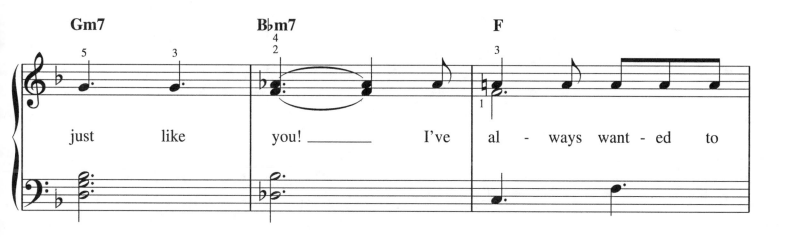

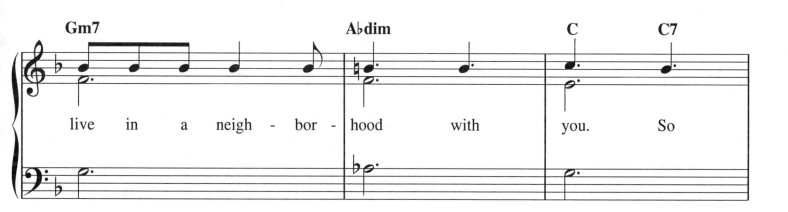

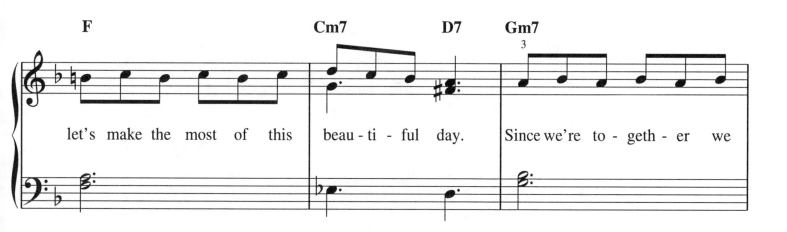

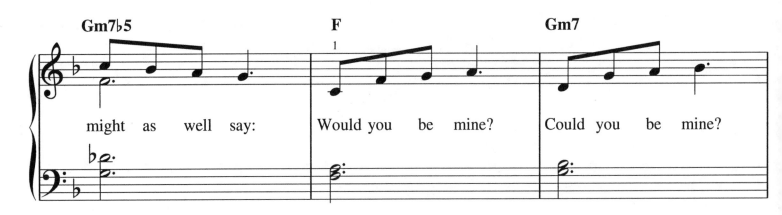

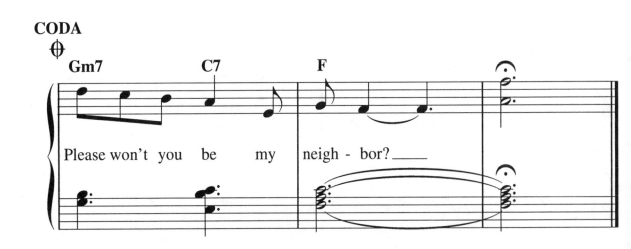